I have known my friend Dr. Phillip M. Davis for almost two decades. The book you hold in your hand is not an idea-come-lately. Challenging men to manhood and investing in younger boys as they transition has been his passion from the very first day I met him.

As I read the book it did three things for me. It brought back memories of men who have been crucial in my life's development—**gratefulness**. It brought to fore areas of my life where I fell short of God's plan for my life as a man—**regrets**. Most importantly, *The Untapped Power of a Man* has challenged me become a wise man—**hope**.

I feel gratefulness and want to do the same for others. I reflect on regrets and promise myself to be the man God wants me to be. I'm hopeful so I can live the rest of my life tapping into the power of a man.

The best thing I like about this book is that while convicting, it's not condemning. I finished the book hopeful, optimistic and with a greater passion to be a difference maker in the lives of men.

—Dr. Sam Chand,
Leadership Consultant and author of Leadership Pain

Whatever a man can be, he must become to be satisfied in life. In Dr. Philip Davis' latest book, *The Untapped Power Of A Man*, he articulates, motivates and navigates men through the maze of manhood to become men of God. Even though this revolutionary book was written for men, it will empower the women who love them. I believe this life-saving resource is the quintessential book on Christlike manhood today!

—Dr. James O. Davis
Cofounder/Billion Soul
Founder/Cutting Edge International
Greater Orlando, Florida

"From the beginning, Man was God's most amazing creation. Different from all other living creatures; man had the ability to think, communicate and operate with skill and precision. He was profound! In this book, there is a unique awakening of the innate power found in the original creation. Far beyond the physical prowess and beauty of men, this book delves deeper--into the mind, heart and soul. Today's culture is in desperate need of men who know who they are and Whose they are! Men...who will function deliberately and consistently to turn the tide of negatives to positives; move from complacency to action; and overcome their weaknesses to operate in power! This book is a valuable catalyst!"

—Dr. Teresa Hairston
Founder/Publisher Emeritus, Gospel Today Magazine
Founder/President, Gospel Heritage Foundation

The Untapped Power of A Man is a divinely ordered message to "Men". In these pages, Dr. Phillip M. Davis masterfully delineates God's description of what a man really is and the divine purpose for which the man was created. Keenly aware of the evils that entrap men and derail their focus from God's intended purpose, Dr. Davis passionately shares founded thoughts that compel men to take their rightful place as responsible fathers, husbands, brothers, businessmen, and to live as men of faith, authority, and purpose.

—Dr. Michael Figgers
Author, Healing The Hearts of Broken Men

"In a time when we need more inspiring stories about the value of a strong family unit, Bishop Davis' book is right on time."

—Michael D. Barnes
Mayor Pro Tem
City of Charlotte

Dr. Phillip Davis in this book *The Untapped Power of A Man* has seen that power at work in people who have developed a culture predicated on respect that could change the negative plight of so many young men and women around us who are running out of options. This book fuels a passion for significance and pulls the pin out of the dynamite of human greatest now couched in the soil of irresponsibility. This book can change a person, a community, a country and a nation. Read it for your edification and share it with your colleagues. It won't be long before it changes you for the better.

—BISHOP LEROY BAILEY, JR.
SENIOR PASTOR
THE FIRST CATHEDRAL BLOOMFIELD, CT.

"Dr. Phillip M. Davis has outdone himself. *The Untapped Power of A Man* speaks poignantly and accurately to the growing crisis of manhood in America. This book provides rich examples and solutions for how to unlock the untapped and undeveloped power within all men. It's a how-to-guide designed to give men the tools, wisdom and support to reclaim their rightful place in society and rise up as the positive force they are designed to be in the earth."

—DR. NITA EVANS, PRESIDENT
SECOND HALF UNIVERSITY

A. W. Tozer once wrote, "Listen to the man who listens to God". The implication here is clear, not every religious communicator is worthy of being heard. Well, you can take comfort in knowing that Dr. Phillip M. Davis is worthy of a listen because his life gives evidence of time spent in the presence of the Almighty. Please read and listen carefully, Dr. Davis in this book has something to say to men and the women who love them.

—GARY L. FROST
VICE PRESIDENT, MIDWEST REGION AND PRAYER
NORTH AMERICAN MISSION BOARD

In a world where positive mental models of manhood are few, it's encouraging to know there's still hope because of the contribution of authors like Dr. Phillip Davis. There is no better teacher than the wisdom and experiences gained by someone who is willing to share and reinvest in others. Davis's latest book entitled *The Untapped Power of A Man* does just that. It realigns, reinforces, reiterates and reveals how integral the man is to achieving God's desire for the family. This book is a gift to this world!

—ALLEN T.D. WIGGINS,

THE HOPE CHURCH, ORLANDO, FL

Bishop Davis persuasively articulates the need for men to view taking responsibility and becoming servant leaders as a blessing to be sought. In so doing, we are engaging the necessary mechanisms for tapping into our dormant potential. Thank you Bishop Davis for this clear-sighted and timely call for men to return to our rightful place of being foundational pillars for rebuilding our society.

—CARNELL JONES

EDUCATION CONSULTANT

"I have been around preaching, preachers and authors for the last 20 years and I can say with all integrity, Bishop Philip Davis is among an elite group of 21st Century communicators. The depth of his personal experience, professional acumen and devotion to the Lord synthesize in the book *The Untapped Power of a Man*. Pastors can draw upon it for wisdom in preaching and counseling, additionally, men in general will be provoked to cultivate and engage their latent potential. Congratulations Bishop Davis on another outstanding work."

—BISHOP MARCUS D. BENJAMIN

THE DANIEL CENTER OF LEADERSHIP

The Untapped Power of A Man is a thought provoking and insightful look at the nature of men and the process of becoming a man of purpose and responsibility. It answers the question, "Am I a real man?"

—JOHN GREGORY

FORMER CHIEF OF POLICE, LAW ENFORCEMENT CONSULTANT

Dr. Davis has given us a blue print on the foundations on what it means to be man.

"What an amazing book, written by one of the brightest minds in the country"

—MARQUES DOUGLAS,
12 YEAR NFL VETERAN AND ENTREPRENEUR

Published by: Billion Soul Publishing
PO Box 623307
Oviedo, FL 32762

ISBN: 978-1-939183-71-2

THE UNTAPPED POWER OF A MAN

THE KEY TO UNLOCKING YOURS

DR. PHILLIP M. DAVIS

with Phillip R.J. Davis

BILLIONSOUL
PUBLISHING

DEDICATION

THIS BOOK IS dedicated to the many great men who serve their families and communities well by living their faith and walking humbly with God. To all those who daily work and strive to be the husbands, fathers, sons, and mentors we need in our world: thank you for being the examples of manhood that God had in mind!

It is quite common today for men to be given a bad rap by our culture and the media. However, I am thankful to the many men who, through the years, have helped positively shape my life. I would not be in a position to salute men of character had it not been for men such as my brothers Robert (deceased), Tony, William, and Rodney.

I have been privileged to have my spiritual life and biblical worldview influenced by such God-fearing and honorable men as the late Dr. E. O. Thomas, Pastor of Inspirational Baptist Church in Cincinnati, Ohio; Pastor William Rorer of Alpha Baptist Church in Bolingbrook, Illinois; and the late Dr. George O. McCalep, Pastor of Greenforest Community Baptist Church in Decatur, Georgia. My leadership lessons have come primarily from the following outstanding leaders and mentors: Dr. Sam Chand, Dr. Richard Harris, and Dr. John Maxwell.

The Bible teaches us to give honor to whom honor is due, and it is my pleasure to recognize these and other men who have impacted my life and helped me along the way.

Also, there are a few other individuals who are my joy and inspiration for living and give my life meaning. Words can't express the depth of my love for Cynthia, my wife of more than forty years, and the gratitude I have to God for this gift who is the queen of my being.

Then there are my sons, Pastor Phillip R. J. Davis and Bradley A. Davis, of whom I can only say as a father that they don't come any better than this. My daughter, Ashley, and my three granddaughters, Jayda, Nicollette, and Camille, continue to motivate me to press toward the mark.

Finally, I dedicate this book to my late father, George; to my late sisters, Elaine, Alfreda, Willa, and Brenda; and to my awesome, beautiful, wise, and wonderful ninety-six-year-old mother, Mamie, the love of my life!

—DR. P. M. DAVIS
CHARLOTTE, NORTH CAROLINA
AUGUST 2015

TABLE OF CONTENTS

FOREWORD

PHILLIP M. DAVIS was known to the world as Bishop, Pastor, Teacher, Leader, Mentor, and much more. I knew him as Father. He passed away on August 29, 2015, just one day before his sixty-third birthday. On that day, I lost the person who believed in me the most. And as the weeks and months pass, I question who, if anyone, can fill that void again as I enter my forties, the prime years of my life.

Although the pain is still fresh, I am encouraged by the fact that my father taught me well. He planted a biblical foundation in me about life, ministry, relationships, and most of all, manhood. He established my identity as a Davis man from my early childhood years. He taught me, just as the Bible says in Proverbs 22:1, that "a good name is to be chosen rather than great riches."He spoke often of the greatness in my life and how I was destined to accomplish great things. He helped me unlock my untapped power as I became the man God called me to be. I'll be the first to say that I am nowhere close to realizing my fullest potential. Like you, I am still on this journey, still a work in progress. However, the confidence I have to succeed lies in what my father passed on to me. That's what this book is about: discovering and unlocking the potential that lies within you. Just as my father recognized the greatness in me, there is greatness in you. Once you began to realize the power that lies within you as a man and release it, your life will never be the same. When I was about ten years old, my father brought home a gift for me. It was a small, plastic, white plaque that cost probably no more than two dollars. However, it wasn't the plaque itself but what it said that was so significant. On this small plastic plaque read the words "Quitters never win...winners never quit." That message has been my driving force throughout life. My dad, with this subtle yet powerful gesture, planted the seed in me that I am a winner, that I am a victor in life. I am not a victim or a quitter, and neither are you. To this day, that two-dollar plaque sits on my desk as a constant reminder that I am a *winner*. In this book, you will discover the untapped power that lies in each and every man and learn how to release it for a life of greatness. You will take a journey through manhood, reflecting on your life, your experiences, and your relationships. You'll unpack biblical principles as you develop a foundation for your life and your family. You'll begin to realize God's standard for manhood and how to not only live according to that standard but pass it on to the next generation.

My father and I both had the opportunity to travel to Kenya, Africa, to participate in missions work. I traveled with a team of nine individuals in 2001, my first mission trip, and again in 2013 with our church's mission team. My father's sole trip was in 2014. Our work was rewarding and life changing because we were able to share the Gospel and see people surrender their lives to Christ. We also had the opportunity to build homes that became local village houses of worship. We shared an unforgettable experience while in Kenya—we were introduced to and interacted with the Maasai, a seminomadic tribe who live in the Serengeti plains of Kenya. We were both able to observe and learn of their culture, their way of living, their relationships among one another, and their spiritual history. The fascinating thing that my father and I both discovered was the uniqueness of the men of the Maasai tribe. As we learned of their journey from boyhood to manhood, we were amazed at the influence these men had in their culture and within their families. How is it that these somewhat primitive people understand and accept the power of manhood, but we in America and other parts of the world have largely missed it? It is with the backdrop of the men of the Maasai tribe that *The*

Untapped Power of a Man comes to life. As my father shares his experience throughout the book, you'll discover that the power is already in you...now it's time to release it.

—PHILLIP R. J. DAVIS, SENIOR PASTOR, NATIONS FORD
COMMUNITY CHURCH
CHARLOTTE, NORTH CAROLINA

INTRODUCTION

THE BACKDROP FOR this book was set on a two-week mission trip to Kenya by sixteen of us from Nations Ford Community Church of Charlotte, North Carolina. I went on this trip to help build houses in Africa and came back having learned something about how to build communities in the United States.

We helped construct several Homes of Hope, providing basic accommodations in Kisumu, west of the capital, Nairobi. The structure of the houses we built in Kenya was not nearly as strong as the most basic houses built in the United States. But I was astonished when I discovered that the community life there was so much stronger and more progressive than ours in many respects. It's funny that I used the word "progressive" to describe their community life because the people I met in Kenya have not changed the way they have built their communities for thousands of years.

What so intrigued me was watching the men of the Maasai tribe go about their daily activities. Serenity permeated the environment as every man understood and embraced his part in the overall success of the village. In more than three decades of serving as a pastor and in various leadership capacities, I have discovered that when a man acknowledges and accepts his role in society—as defined by God rather than by the world around him—he is productive and at peace.

Success and peace in so many societies are, for the most part, mutually exclusive terms, with many men having neither—but not so with the Maasai. They seem to instinctively get that manhood doesn't begin in the gym or on the playing field, but in the soul. They understand that manhood is not instantaneous, but a journey on which a boy breaks free from his mother and finds his father. They temper their pride and competiveness with a strong commitment to their responsibility to society. In so many ways, they just seem to get it!

> Success and peace in so many societies are, for the most part, mutually exclusive terms, with many men having neither—but not so with the Maasai. They seem to instinctively get that manhood doesn't begin in the gym or on the playing field, but in the soul.

But this is not exclusive to the Maasai. I believe that what they have tapped into is deeply embedded within every man created by God, regardless of his culture or country of origin. It is there for those living in *kraals* in Kenya or rented apartments in cities and suburbs across the United States, for men who follow their livestock on foot and men who fly to business meetings chasing the next deal.

If in this book I can convey just a fraction of what was deposited in my spirit while on this trip, then I will have accomplished my goal.

It is critical that men learn to cut their mother's apron strings and identify with their fathers and other men who can lead and prepare them for the responsibilities of manhood. Just as the Maasai boys embrace manhood, we must create an environment in which becoming a man is celebrated and encouraged, not fundamentally discouraged. Without that passage, chances are, men will continue to follow the misguided voice of their inner child.

> It is critical that men learn to cut their mother's apron strings and identify with their fathers and other men who can lead and prepare them for the responsibilities of manhood.

This book is for men and the women who love and encourage them. It is my desire that through this reading, men will be challenged and learn to unlock the untapped power that is within.

Chapter One

THE PERVADER: OBSERVING THE MAASAI

WE CONCLUDED OUR trip with a three-day safari into the Serengeti region, a vast area that spans twelve thousand square miles from Kenya to its neighbor, Tanzania. The Serengeti is known as one of the greatest areas for wildlife in the world. It was thrilling to see lions, zebras, impalas, and other exotic animals in their natural habitat. National Geographic Channel programs are wonderful, but they can't begin to capture what we experienced from actually being there.

While I was overwhelmed by the breadth and beauty of the region, I was impacted even more by the tribal people we came into contact with. The highlight of our safari was a trip to the homeland of the Maasai tribe, the semi-nomadic people who make that part of the region their home.

We were welcomed warmly into their simple community, called a *kraal,* which is made up of a large number of round huts surrounded by hand-woven fences protecting humans and livestock from predators. We were greeted with traditional singing and dancing. I could not stop laughing as I participated in the Maasai men's jumping dance called the *adumu,* in which the height of your jumps determine how many wives you are considered worthy to take. I was told that my efforts meant I could have two; however, rest assured, my wife, Cynthia, is all I ever need or want! Afterward, we ducked and squeezed into an *Inkajijik,* a small, dried-dung-and-thatch hut, to sit and visit.

They didn't have much in the way of possessions, compared even to many of our poorest communities in America, but there was a quiet strength that intrigued me. These people were content living without the many consumer trappings of western culture that we deem indispensable to life. However, despite their meager lifestyle, the Maasai had something more: a peace and a power within that caused them to live with a sense of unity and purpose.

From our narrow perspective, communities in the United States seem to have it all together. There are well-developed neighborhoods, good roads, and lots of public amenities. There is an orderly place for everything, and everything is in its place. In contrast, the Maasai seemed at first glance to live rather randomly. There are no measured plots, organized streets, or well-placed trees. But as I looked more closely, I came to see much greater order and purpose there than in many places I knew back home. I discovered that while Maasai villages appear to be unorganized and haphazardly built from the outside, there is a clear structure inside every home. Conversely, many American homes that look great from the outside are unfortunately chaotic on the inside.

The more I saw, the more questions I had for my Maasai hosts. For example, I was intrigued by the inner and outer fences surrounding their village. Why two circular fences? The outer thorny fence is their initial wall of defense from predators, I learned. The inner one, I was told, was where the young boys would round up the livestock and cattle each night and keep them secure and safe from predators, especially lions, that at times would break through the outer fence.

Noticing that the Maasai men tended to be tall, I wanted to know why the huts stood so low—the average hut was a shade under five feet, requiring the men to stoop when they entered.

"The huts aren't built for the men," I was told. I must have looked puzzled because my guide added, "The huts are built for the women and children, and they are smaller. The men stay outside, to protect everyone else."

There was only one narrow entrance into the hut, forcing us to squeeze in slowly after each other. Inside, less than two feet from the opening, was a hardened manure wall that further impeded progress. It all seemed a bit awkward, I thought.

"We build this way for protection," I was told. "If a lion manages to break through the outer fence, he will first come to the huts, but it's not easy for him to get into one of them. Lions can be quite large, so they find it difficult to turn or maneuver in tight spaces. That would give all the women and children just enough time to escape through one of the small windows in their sleeping area."

I found myself amazed by the culture. I was fascinated with how they interacted with each other. There was something different about the men that captured my attention. There was a unique quality about them, something I could not put my finger on, that kept calling and drawing me closer.

Then I made the connection, and immediately, my mind went back to my childhood in Cincinnati, Ohio, half a century ago, when children were taught by the men of my community to respect their elders and young boys looked up to the men in their lives. Then I thought about how different things are these days in cities and suburbs today across the United States.

I began asking our safari guide all about the Maasai culture, especially about the role of the men in the community. Their presence stirred something within me, and my curiosity increased the more I observed them. I noticed the way they walked and talked among themselves, the playfulness they had with one another, and the extraordinary respect they gave to their leaders and elders.

The quality in the Maasai that captured my attention more than anything was this internal power of peace that seemed to influence and impact every aspect of their lives—their family, community, and business relationships, and ultimately their spiritual relationships.

Something was staring me right in the face, but I simply could not see it at the time. What was it? What was the unique, powerful influence these Maasai men had on their social environment that energized my inner man? I began to ask myself the question, "What can we learn from the men living in this society that will benefit our families, communities, and nations?"

> The quality in the Maasai that captured my attention more than anything was this internal power of peace that seemed to influence and impact every aspect of their lives—their family, community, and business relationships, and ultimately their spiritual relationships.

Again, I found myself reflecting on some of the men in my life, and on my relationship with my own father. I recalled the times when there was a calming peace in our home—there was no doubt that this was driven by Dad's presence, even if we did not hear his voice. I believe this powerful peace can be felt in any home when a father understands and walks in the role and purpose for which he was created.

As I continued to think about what I had experienced during our visit with the Maasai, I noticed that this extraordinary force the men exhibited was not limited to the biological fathers of the village. It was apparent that all of the men seemed to exhibit the same unwavering strength. Perhaps, it occurred to me, it might be an inherent, untapped quality within every man—one that simply needs to be unlocked through teaching, training, discovery, and development.

Mind you, there were some crude, even disturbing things about the Maasai culture that I did not care for. Their practice of female genital mutilation, for example, has been the focus of much well-deserved international criticism. Also, women are typically treated as property, and if a young girl gets pregnant before marriage, she is ostracized and permanently banished from her village.

Not everything is rosy in the world of the Maasai, to be sure. However, it appears that the men have wisely built into their culture a social framework that promotes certain specific values similar to those found in the Bible. Indeed, some Maasai believe that they are actually one of the ten lost tribes of Israel.

AN ECHO OF THE OLD TESTAMENT

When you line up the beliefs, cultural customs, and rituals of the Maasai with the tribes of Israel, some astonishing similarities jump out at you.

First, the Israelites and the Maasai believe in one God that is omnipotent and omnipresent. The Maasai call their one God Ngai or Enkai, while the Israealites refer to Yahweh.

Second, the Israelites divide a person's life into four stages: from birth to age five, age five to twenty, age twenty to sixty, and from age sixty on. In Leviticus 27:1–8, we read how different monetary values were established based on a male's potential work capacity. Similarly, the Maasai divide a person's life into five age sets that are determined not by age but by the transition of older age groups to different age sets. The Maasai stages are from birth to pre-circumcision, from circumcision to junior warrior, from junior warrior to senior warrior, from senior warrior to junior elder, and from junior elder to senior elder. A social or economic value is established for each age set.

The Israelites gave important responsibilities to their young boys; for example, Old Testament figures Joseph and David were responsible for herding their family's livestock. In the same kind of way, Maasai boys are typically responsible for tending their family's herds and flocks, their primary source of wealth.

A fourth Israelite–Maasai connection is that young Israelites twenty years old or more were required to serve in Israel's army,

THE UNTAPPED POWER OF A MAN

as we see in Numbers 1:45. Once circumcised, Maasai boys immediately become junior warriors and are required to protect their village.

Finally, for both the Israelites and the Maasai, circumcision is believed necessary to maintain their covenant with God.

With such similarities, it appears that the basis for much of the behavior of the Maasai men from birth through adulthood is rooted in the cultural customs of God's chosen people, the Israelites.

AN UNTAPPED POTENTIAL

For the rest of my brief time in Kenya, I became a human sponge, soaking up the culture and asking countless questions of our tour guide. As a leader of men and founder of the Male Leadership Academy for boys in Charlotte, I wanted to know about the young boys and the men in particular. What I learned caused me to examine the culture and the community of men I know.

My time among the Maasai helped me come to a greater understanding of some of the keys to unlocking the untapped power that is within a man.

I believe this resource is to be found within every man created by God, regardless of his culture or country of origin. It is there for those living in *kraals* in Kenya or rented apartments in cities and suburbs across the United States, for men who follow their livestock on foot and men who fly to business meetings chasing the next deal.

> In more than three decades of serving as a pastor and in various leadership roles, I have discovered that when a man acknowledges and accepts his role in society—as defined by God rather than by the world around him—he is at peace.

While there are some men who are only at peace with either nature, their fellow man, or their Creator, there are few men who are at peace with all three.

Becoming a man does not begin in the gym; it begins in the soul. Nor is it instantaneous. It is a journey, a process. For a boy to become a man, he must first break free from his mother and find his father.

The Maasai embed the transition from boy to man through public pronouncements and rituals. A young Maasai boy begins his journey to manhood by first tending to the cattle. This includes keeping predators away and milking the cattle daily. When the boy's father believes his son is ready, he formally approaches the tribe's religious leader to ask for his blessing to have his son circumcised.

Once the Maasai boy is selected to be initiated into manhood, he goes through a precircumcision ceremony called *Enkipaata*. A Maasai youth is expected to lie silent and stoic as his most private skin is cut and salt is rubbed into the wound. Any movement or sound is considered to be a sign of weakness and will be met with ridicule and embarrassment.

American youth desperately need some milestone event signaling their transition from adolescence to manhood. Though a serious life event for the Maasai, I caught myself smirking for a moment as I thought about how quickly the idea of suggesting a similar ritual for young men in the United States would be dismissed.

Not that I would disagree, but part of the problem we have in America is that countless men have never cut their mother's apron strings; thus, they have never found their father or a father figure who could lead them into manhood. As a result, these boys are not prepared to handle the responsibilities that come with manhood.

Just as the Maasai boys embrace manhood, we must create an environment in which becoming a man is celebrated and encouraged, not fundamentally discouraged. Without that passage, chances are, a man will forever be guided by the voice of his inner child.

We need to learn how to grow boys into men.

> Just as the Maasai boys embrace manhood, we must create an environment in which becoming a man is celebrated and encouraged, not fundamentally discouraged. Without that passage, chances are, a man will forever be guided by the voice of his inner child.

Chapter Two

THE PROBLEM: MEANDERING MEN

THE MAASAI DO not draw attention to themselves, but I noticed the time and effort they put into the training and developing of their boys to become men of responsibility. Our African guide told me that the Maasai men rotate shifts, staying up all night, in the still darkness of the Serengeti, with no one around and no one to talk with. They stay alert in rotation, protecting the village from lions and other dangerous predators. Their lives are filled with purpose. The adult Maasai men are the unseen foundation on which their society is built which prompted my safari guide to say, "Their children do not get in trouble. They have no problems out of their children."

Because of the time and energy spent teaching their young boys the tribe's history, culture, and customs, the Maasai develop men who understand and eagerly accept their roles and responsibilities. Every man is prepared to take on the many challenges that may come their way. It is not by accident that they are effective problem solvers as opposed to being the cause of problems.

The Maasai women are also well aware of their roles. They are described as the backbone of their communities. Together, these men and women resisted the attempts by British Colonialists and the Kenyan government to force them to become more aligned with modern culture. The unity the Maasai men have with their women is the primary reason their ancient culture has survived for centuries. The men are sure of their place and purpose—in marked contrast to many other parts of the world.

THE NEW NORMAL

Consider several of the past and present crises impacting the United States—the terrorist attacks of September 11, 2001; multiple school shooting massacres; the 2008 recession; or the rising heroin epidemic. Major life-changing events such as these prompt intensive counter-responses to rectify the situation and ensure that the problem doesn't get worse or happen again. Left unaddressed, each of these crises will become a condition. And in due time, that condition will become the culture. A material event, or sequence of such events, can become a way of life when not addressed in a meaningful way.

> B ecause of the time and energy spent teaching their young boys the tribe's history, culture, and customs, the Maasai develop men who understand and eagerly accept their roles and responsibilities.

This is exactly what is happening with respect to masculinity. Men in Western society have been under attack from extreme forms of feminism, with no systematic attempt to push back. Thus, we have gone from crisis to condition to culture, and men are going through their entire lives not understanding what it means to be a man, or what it means to be truly masculine. This has become the new normal.

What are some of the results of this crisis–condition–culture pattern with regard to men? I can remember when "men were men." The traditional male roles gave men a sense of identity and purpose and brought a degree of stability from generation to generation. However, along the way something changed, and the role of men began to be challenged aggressively.

Candidly, I believe some type of change was necessary, as men broadly failed for too long to treat women with the love and respect God has commanded. However, what began as a noble initiative to give women the rights they deserved became an all-out assault on men. Over time, feminists fine-tuned their focus on blurring one of the core characteristics that defines men: masculinity.

This shift away from traditional views of masculinity created a crisis in identity for men in general. They began to question who they were and what roles they should play in life. While continuing to work, marry, have families, and follow their pursuits in life, many men lost touch with what it really meant to be a man, a husband, or a father.

Over time, the change in attitudes toward masculinity by both men and women caused the crisis in masculine identity to become a condition that gained social and political traction, with little or no opposition from anyone—including the family-focused Christian community. Consequently, men have willingly accepted this new normal. The advent of the "metrosexual" and the movement toward gender neutrality are a just two examples of how this identity crisis has manifested as a serious effort to totally redefine masculinity.

What have been the results of this shift around the world? According to pastor and Bible teacher Myles Munroe, "The male holds the key to the nations, and our nations are in crisis."[1]

The great British preacher John Wesley once said, "What one generation tolerates, the next generation will embrace."[2] The book of Judges recounts how, following the death of Joshua and his trusted leaders, the culture shifted to one of weakness and disobedience.

Judges 2:10–12 (NKJV) notes, "When all that generation had been gathered to their fathers, another generation arose after them who did not know the Lord nor the work which He had done for Israel. Then the children of Israel did evil in the sight of the Lord, and served the Baals; and they forsook the Lord God of their fathers...."

When men lose their masculine identity and sense of

purpose, they lose their way and seek to cope with their emptiness in unproductive ways.

Throughout the world, who is responsible for the most crime? Who makes up most of the prison population? Who is more likely to be involved in drug trafficking and drug abuse? Who, typically, are the primary gang members? Who is more likely to be carriers of the AIDS virus?

> When men lose their masculine identity and sense of purpose, they lose their way and seek to cope with their emptiness in unproductive ways.

The answer each and every time is men.

An article in the *Electronic Journal of Sociology* titled "Masculinity and Crime" by Jessie L. Krienert of Illinois State University, noted that "Men with high masculinity and few acceptable outlets to assert masculinity are more likely to be in a violent incident. These findings suggest the need for better measures of both masculinity and the appropriate outlets for masculine expression."[3]

THE NEW CULTURAL REALITIES

There are many other areas in which men are facing serious problems as a result of our shifting culture. I recently came across an article that listed "Ten Examples of Men's Issues the Media Love to Ignore,"[4] which I will summarize:

1. Violence. From the time they are little boys who are taught to be aggressive and "fight back," men are more prone to violence. Not only are they more likely to be the perpetrators, despite all the right and proper concern about violence against women, men are more frequently

the victims—of violent crimes, gang attacks, and prison assaults. Boys are more likely to be beaten up and bullied in school than girls.

2. Depression. Though most studies indicate that women actually are more likely to suffer anxiety or depression than men, females are also more likely to seek help and counseling and treatment. Men tend to suffer in silence. Great actors, they can be good at pretending nothing is wrong, even while they are dying on the inside: suicide is recognized as a leading cause of death among men and boys.

3. Unemployment. Studies show a vast gender gap in education, with men trailing women by a growing margin in pretty much all areas of attainment. Sixty percent of all bachelor's degrees in America are held by women, creating a tremendous challenge for men when it comes to finding work. The jobless rate for black male dropouts, for example, now stands at more than 50 percent. According to the *Los Angeles Times*, only about half of all boys expect to work in well-paid professional jobs when they grow up, compared to nearly three-quarters of girls.

4. Income disparity. Women earn, on average, only 80 percent of what men do—but that's not the whole story. Researchers who looked at workers' pay in 150 of the biggest US cities found that unmarried, childless women under thirty made, on average, 8 percent more than their male equivalents. In Atlanta and Memphis, that gap stretched to 20 percent more; in New York, it was 17 percent. The main reason: women as a

group were more qualified, so they had greater earning potential.

5. Abuse. Many headlines tend to center on violence in the home against women, and it is clearly a significant problem I am in no way trying to minimize. But men can be victims, too. Forty percent of all UK domestic violence victims were male, according to one study, according to *The Guardian*. Yet there are only thirty-three beds in men's shelters in the entire country, compared with four thousand spaces for women. Compounding the issue, male police officers are often unsympathetic to male abuse victims, leading to a frighteningly low conviction rate, even by domestic violence standards.

6. Cancer. Pink power is clear—breast cancer research attracts more funding than any other kind. Every dollar spent there is to be welcomed, of course, but we need to see an equal amount being raised for prostate cancer research. After all, the risks involved are nearly identical. The National Cancer Institute reports that one in eight women will face breast cancer in their lifetimes, while one in seven men will develop prostate cancer.

7. Danger. Men account for 93 percent of all workplace deaths in America. That is a rather disproportionate ratio when you factor in that women clock around 43 percent of all the hours worked each year. But it is because blue-collar men tend to work the most dangerous jobs. Fishermen, loggers, and truck drivers have the highest fatality rates in the country.

8. Homelessness. Seven out of ten of those out on the streets in a 2007 survey conducted for the US mayors' congress were men. That rate is even higher in other parts of the world; 88 percent of the homeless in a random survey in Amsterdam were men. If men are more likely to find themselves on the street, they also fare less well there. A Danish report noted that homeless men die an average of five years earlier than homeless women.

9. Separation. Women win sole-custody battles five out of six times, according to a 2008 report by *Newsweek*. That is because many judges hold to the view that women should be at home with their children while the men are out bringing back a paycheck. "This leads to a strange state of affairs," the online article observed, "where men are often automatically considered to be a bad parent, even in cases where they're demonstrably not."

10. Our own notions of masculinity. The writer concluded his list of "hidden" problems faced by men with this one, which he says is most damaging of all. He said this:

> As fathers, we teach boys to lash out instead of restrain themselves. As a culture we teach men to hide their emotions even if it kills them. As a society we teach boys to aim low and not educate themselves for a well-paying job. And this masculinity confusion has gotten us: a propensity for suicide, prone to homelessness, often unable to see our kids and unwilling to confront violence with anything but more violence.

Our blindness to the major issues men face in the world today is complicated by two factors. First, it's not easy for men to talk about these issues because most men would rather suffer in silence than admit to having problems they do not know how to deal with. Second, even when men are willing to open up, many of the issues are not addressed because our culture has become so sensitive about the idea of there being any fundamental differences between men and woman. It's just not politically correct. I begrudgingly refer to this condition men are facing as Chronic Masculinity Crisis, or "CMC."

THE ROOT CAUSE OF CMC

The reality is that many men are suffering from a lack of masculine identity. As a result they are limping through life, disillusioned and frustrated. As Dr. Bill Winston, Senior Pastor of Living Word Christian Center of Forest Park, Illinois, said, "The problem facing men worldwide is not a biological one of maleness, but a spiritual one of identity."[5] If the mark or measure of a man is his willingness to accept and shoulder responsibility, then his ability to do so is rooted in his having a firm, solid, true identity.

It is true for all of us that one of the critical roles of a father—indeed of all men—is to help the next generation discover and develop their identity. When men do not give their children a clear sense of who they are, their daughters may seek affirmation and identity from the wrong sources, including boyfriends, TV, and social media rather than the Bible. And when men do not give their sons a sense of their male identity, they just might seek it in a gang or in some other misguided social activities.

The issue of masculine identity simply cannot be understated. Every man longs to have someone who believes in him and is willing to invest in his life. Because boys do not automatically become men with age, there is the need for their fathers or male role models to mentor them through the journey into manhood.

When on his death bed, King David told Solomon, his son, "Be strong and show yourself a man," (1 Kings 2:2, ESV) he was instilling in him the need for responsibility, and to be totally identified with his manhood. Solomon had to look back over his time spent with his father and recall the journey. Then he had to make the choice to be responsible for what his father had instilled in him, and to identify with the values, courage, and character that had been modeled for him.

> Because boys do not automatically become men with age, there is the need for their fathers or male role models to mentor them through the journey into manhood.

So it is with every man. Each of us has to choose to take the steps necessary to grow up. Like the Maasai boys, we have to face pain and fear as we move into manhood. Along that journey are steps requiring training and discipline. With each step comes greater responsibility—because the older you get as a man, the more your mistakes cost!

What are those steps, and what are the traits that can help a man be clear about his identity? How do you know when you have successfully made the transition from boyhood to adolescence to manhood to mentor to sage?

In his book *Wild at Heart*, John Eldredge identifies five stages in a man's life. In a follow-up book, he adds a sixth stage.[6] In his work *The Masculine Journey*, Robert Hicks also identifies six stages of manhood.[7] More recently, author and leadership expert Tim Elmore identified four specific steps along the journey of masculinity, in a blog titled "LeBron James: The Four Stages of Manhood."[8]

Though these writers may divide the stages differently, they focus on similar themes and issues. Let me offer a compromise by sharing what I believe are five critical steps or stages along the journey to manhood.

Stage	Age	Characteristic
Boyhood	0–11 years	Explorer
Adolescence	12–20 years	Warrior
Manhood	21–40 years	Lover
Mentor	41–60 years	Father
Sage	61-plus years	Wise man

You will notice that each stage along the way involves the choice to be more responsible, though this is perhaps most clearly seen when someone transitions from adolescence to manhood. It is here that a young man must then learn the lesson that the Apostle Paul taught in 1 Corinthians 13:11 (NKJV): "When I was a child, I spoke as a child, I understood as a child, I thought as a child; but when I became a man, I put away childish things."

Education expert and consultant Dr. Jawanza Kunjufu has stated, "There is a difference between a male, a boy, and a man. A person is born male. He grows into a boy, and a boy likes to play. Young boys play with cars and trucks. Old boys play with women and their children. Men are responsible. They work before they play."9

The stage from adolescence to manhood is the most critical and vulnerable period of time in the development of a man's identity. Many men struggle during this stage because they are faced with the responsibilities of being a man and the fear of leaving adolescence, where they have lived wild and free. This is the time in his life when a man is at his peak in terms of physical strength, stamina, and thinking capacity.

If he does not understand that this stage between adolescence and manhood is potentially the time for his greatest opportunities and achievements, he can hold on to adolescence too long. In fact, many men get confused during this transition and remain in the adolescence stage well into their forties and fifties. Uncertain and unwilling to take on responsibility, they remain boys in men's bodies. They just change the nature and cost of their toys!

> The stage from adolescence to manhood is the most critical and vulnerable period of time in the development of a man's identity. Many men struggle during this stage because they are faced with the responsibilities of being a man and the fear of leaving adolescence, where they have lived wild and free.

So this time of greatest potential is also all too often the time when a man is most prone to his greatest failures. It is vital that he gets help along the way. He needs a father figure, a mentor who can help him navigate between adolescence and manhood.

Once safely through this transition, he can then turn to the younger ones behind him and become the mentor or sage who, in turn, guides them through this difficult time in their lives.

THE ULTIMATE EXAMPLE

For men to understand and truly embrace their masculinity, they must first understand man's relationship with God. God designed and intentionally gave man certain physical and mental characteristics needed for His good pleasure and for His will to be done. More specifically, He made man different from women in accordance with His divine purpose for this world, and no social or political movement can change that. While certain physical differences enable procreation, men and women also differ in many other ways, for example in terms of muscle mass, brain size, and bone structure.

Men exhibit less emotion and excel at various spatial skills, while women excel in verbal fluency and have greater memory for objects. The differences between men and women vary, but what is important for us to recognize is that structural and cognitive differences between genders are real and intentional.

Mind you, these differences do not make men or women superior or inferior to one another; *they make them the perfect complement to each other.*

God made man to lead, protect, provide, and sacrifice. He made woman to be supportive, courageous, understanding, and to give life. When they come together as husband and wife, it creates a perfect picture of God's relationship with us.

The ultimate example of masculinity and how it should be embraced can be found by examining the life of Jesus Christ. His actions were not what we would expect of a "masculine man," but that is because we have a worldly mind-set. He was not macho, prideful, domineering, cocky, or competitive. On the contrary, Jesus was and is powerful yet gentle, commanding but not condescending, loving, consistent, dependable, confident, humble, faithful, prayerful, and eternal-minded.

There are many other adjectives I could use to describe Christ, but hopefully by now you can see the contrast between the secular and spiritual view of masculinity. God designed men to have a balance of strength, leadership, love, faith, and servitude; this combination is the essence of masculinity.

With that in mind, men will continue to suffer from CMC until they make a heartfelt commitment to follow Christ. In doing so, godly men will have an earnest desire to celebrate their God-given masculinity.

> God designed men to have a balance of strength, leadership, love, faith, and servitude; this combination is the essence of masculinity.

Chapter Three

THE PINNACLE: EMBRACING FATHER GOD

THERE IS A place all men need to come to if they ever want to release their untapped power, if they ever want to be all they can be and all their families and communities need them to be. They need to start from a position of submission and safety. They need to start with God as Father, knowing the Creator God as their heavenly Father.

Unfortunately, in much of the modern world the once-revered position of father, or an adult man, has been diminished by the media. In many movies and TV shows, fathers are portrayed as being absent or absent-minded—well-meaning, maybe, but essentially clueless. Sadly, too many men in the real world have given good reasons for this unflattering portrayal.

REDEFINING FATHERHOOD

History tells us that the post-World War II economic expansion was one of the greatest periods in American history. It was followed by the Vietnam War and the oil crisis of the seventies, then the economic boom of the nineties. These were the wonder years for the baby boomers.

What is not said about my generation is that we ushered in an era of greed, drugs, abortion, and a host of other things that negatively impacted our culture. We were gaining wealth at breathtaking speed, and as a result, men became married to their jobs. Spending time with our children meant a quick chat before giving them money to go shopping at the mall.

We missed our children's extracurricular activities and parent–teacher meetings. We were in and out of marriages in less time than it took to order a burger and fries. The media began to glorify men who had money. Quite simply, the men of my generation equated being a good father and husband with their net worth. This resulted in children growing up with a father who was around physically but checked out emotionally and mentally. It also resulted in the highest divorce rate this country has ever experienced, not to mention the corporate greed that led to a host of white-collar crimes.

> Quite simply, the men of my generation equated being a good father and husband with their net worth. This resulted in children growing up with a father who was around physically but checked out emotionally and mentally.

THE PERFECT FATHER–SON RELATIONSHIP

To reverse this negative portrayal of men, we need to first look at the relationship of the heavenly Father with His earthly Son. Their love for and honor of one another gives us a model for all human fathers and for all men as they relate to their families and their communities.

Before you build a tall building, you need to lay a firm foundation. Before you set out on a long journey, you need a road map so that you head in the right direction. You need to know your starting place. Before you can really be a man, or a father, you need to know what it means to be a son.

Jesus's relationship with His Father presents a perfect example of how men should relate to God, and in turn how children should relate to their fathers. Jesus's obedience to His Father's will, His passionate love for His Father, and His personal reflection of His Father's nature stand as a testament to all men who seek to be true sons of God.

GOD IS FATHER

The crowd that gathered on the hillside in northern Israel must have been pretty excited. Here was the man they had heard so much about. The one who spoke so powerfully and who had been performing miracles was there to tell them more about God. As He delivered what would become known as the Sermon on the Mount, Jesus chose a most unusual word for God. He said, "Let your light shine before men in such a way that they may see your good works and glorify your Father who is in heaven" (Matt. 5:16, NASB).

> Jesus's obedience to His Father's will, His passionate love for His Father, and His personal reflection of His Father's nature stand as a testament to all men who seek to be true sons of God.

Father? Did He say "Father"? No doubt there was a stir among the people as they asked one another if they had heard correctly. Was He referring to the awesome God of the Jewish nation? What a strange term to use for the Almighty, the God who had thundered forth His purposes from Mount Sinai and established the Jewish people as a nation.

Other names were more familiar to the Jews of Jesus's day: Elohim, Yahweh, El Elyon, Adonai, Jehovah, and El Shaddai. These were some of the sacred Hebraic titles ascribed to the God of Israel that elicited awe and reverence. God's infrequent appearances or revelation of Himself in Israel's history only enhanced the mystery surrounding Him.

Shrouded in transcendent glory, unapproachable by man— very few in the chronicles of Jewish literature could claim to have personally encountered the Most High God. Who could ever think of ascending to the lofty places where God dwells and return with a knowledge of the Most High? And if you did, how would you describe Him? What word would best communicate His majestic presence and nature? Coming from His endless time with God, stepping into our world, Jesus used the word "Father." This was no careless mistake or isolated incident. In His historic address on the mountainside, Jesus used the word fifteen times. Among them:

- "But you, when you pray, go into your inner room, close your door, and pray to your Father who is in secret, and your Father who sees what is done in secret will reward you" (Matt. 6:6, NASB).

- "Your Father knows what you need, before you ask Him" (Matt. 6:8, NASB).

Perhaps most famously, when He instructed His followers how to pray, Jesus told them, "Pray, then, in this way: 'Our Father who is in heaven, Hallowed be Your name'" (Matt. 6:9, NASB).

Throughout His ministry, Jesus would consistently use the word "Father," a distinctively masculine term, when communicating. The Gospel of John records the word more than ninety times. This title superseded all previous revelations of God. One of the main thrusts of Jesus's mission on earth was to reconcile mankind to God their Father.

We need to understand that Jesus was not merely looking for a word that would help man know and interpret God. He was not offering an anthropological model to explain the unexplainable. In using the word "Father," in its most sublime and noble sense, He was declaring the essence of who and what God is and to what every man, every earthly father, should aspire.

Fatherhood is intrinsic to God's nature and unique to His relationship with the creation. Out of His Father-heart, mankind was birthed. In Him, and only in Him, all men can find true significance. On one occasion near the end of His earthly ministry, in the upper room, one of Jesus's followers asked something that still echoes through the corridors of time. Philip said, "Lord, show us the Father, and it is enough for us" (John 14:8–9, ESV). Jesus replied, "Have I been with you so long, and you still do not know me, Philip? Whoever has seen me has seen the Father."

Jesus was profoundly disappointed that Philip had not yet grasped this vital point He had emphasized so much. Philip had been one of Jesus's first followers, walking with Him for three years. He had heard the words, seen the works, and felt His nearness, yet he had failed to comprehend Jesus's life purpose.

CLOSE TO THE FATHER

I always felt close to my father, something that was unique coming from where I grew up. The other so-called fathers in my old neighborhood mostly checked in and then checked out. Unfortunately, many men have never felt the affection of a father or a caring father figure. They rarely, if ever, had a one-on-one, heart-to-heart conversation where their father showed real interest in them.

When fathers spoke to their sons back then, it was usually to give instructions or to criticize something they did wrong. Do either of these sound familiar to you? "I need you to mow the lawn—and do it right this time." "You think going to school makes you smarter than me?"

These fathers found it more difficult to simply say something positive to their children than to work back-to-back ten-hour shifts at their jobs. Most of the time, I found that a good number of these fathers really loved their children, but they never learned how to communicate with them. In most instances, the fathers of these men were not around or did not communicate with them effectively when they were younger. This adverse trend created a significant communication gap between men and their loved ones. Hopefully, recognizing this will help some of you who are still frustrated with your fathers understand them better and reconcile your differences.

When you think about how often God expressed His love and encouragement to His Son, Jesus, there should be no surprise about Jesus's feelings toward His Father. He displayed an intense passion for His Father from an early age. The year He turned twelve, Jesus went with Mary and Joseph on their customary pilgrimage to Jerusalem so they could celebrate the Feast of Passover. But this time, while on their way home, they realized that Jesus was not with them.

Frantically hurrying back to the city, they searched every conceivable corner for their son. Finally, after three days, they located Him in the temple, talking with the priests as their equal. By this time most likely exhausted from fear and worry, Mary spoke harshly as she questioned Jesus's treatment of His parents.

Jesus the God-man turned to her and with what seems to have been a mixture of calmness and perplexity and asked, "Why did you seek Me? Did you not know that I must be about My Father's business?" (Luke 2:49, NKJV). The literal Greek here reads, "Did you not know that I must be (busy) in the (affairs) of My Father?"

This powerful, passionate conviction would distinguish Jesus's life. In the heart of Jesus Christ, the Incarnate Son, there was a determination and a drive to accomplish the Father's work and to reveal His Father's ways, in the short time available to Him. This is the passion every man must develop, the same passion to know his creator intimately and personally.

Jesus's passion for the Father was founded on His uniqueness as the only Son of the Father. In His pre-incarnate existence, He was the darling Son of Father God, the "apple of His eye." As the "only Son," He enjoyed a depth of relationship with His Father that was beyond the scope and comprehension of the human mind.

> In the heart of Jesus Christ, the Incarnate Son, there was a determination and a drive to accomplish the Father's work and to reveal His Father's ways, in the short time available to Him. This is the passion every man must develop, the same passion to know his creator intimately and personally.

John 1:18 (NKJV) reads, "No one has seen God at any time. The only begotten Son, who is in the bosom of the Father, He has declared Him." "In the bosom of another" was an ancient near-Eastern phrase used to describe a very personal and tender relationship. It denoted intimacy, friendship, and affection. Jesus's intimate experience of God transcended any cerebral knowledge the Jewish leaders may have had. It came from this most intimate place.

THE FATHER'S AFFIRMATION

Jesus's passion to please His Father was fueled by the profound love between the two of them. The Bible makes it clear that Jesus loves the Father and that the Father deeply loves His Son:

- "The Father loves the Son and has given all things into His hand" (John 3:35, NASB).

- "For the Father loves the Son, and shows Him all things that He Himself is doing; and the Father will show Him greater works than these, so that you will marvel" (John 5:20, NASB).

From this great love relationship between God and the God-man, Jesus, we get a glimpse of the possibility of the relationship between human fathers and sons.

One of the basic needs of a man is encouragement. When a father loves his son, he is quick to encourage him. When Jesus was baptized by John in the River Jordan, as He came up out of the water, the voice of God the Father could be heard saying, "This is My beloved Son, in whom I am well pleased" (Matt. 3:17, NKJV).

Can you imagine the adrenaline that must have shot through Jesus's veins and the look on His face to hear His father publicly pronounce that He was proud of and pleased with Him? When a man receives that kind of encouragement, he can unlock reserves of untapped power that propel him to accomplish his goals.

Jesus went into the wilderness and faced the devil, going without food or water for forty days and forty nights. On the strength of the encouragement He received from His father, Jesus accomplished one of the most challenging tasks He would ever face.

This is the most basic of all our missions, the fundamental assignment of our lives: to make sure our children know that we love them. To say to each son, "I'm proud of you. You have what it takes." To let each daughter know, "How I delight in you. You are so lovely." We'll have done a pretty good job if we can frequently and consistently say this over the course of their childhood.

The power of a father's love can never be underestimated because it is in this loving atmosphere that the fresh air of confidence, security, and destiny is breathed into every child. It is also in this love that correction and restitution find their ultimate purpose.

I have always tried to encourage my sons openly, publicly sharing with them and with others how proud and pleased I am with them. They have never given me any trouble, never been in trouble with the law, never fathered children out of wedlock; they graduated from college, and both, of their own choosing, have joined me in ministry.

> The power of a father's love can never be underestimated because it is in this loving atmosphere that the fresh air of confidence, security, and destiny is breathed into every child. It is also in this love that correction and restitution find their ultimate purpose.

WELCOMING THE PRODIGAL SON

One of the most famous of Jesus's stories, compellingly and compassionately illustrating the loving heart of Father God, is in Luke 15:11–32. This story is traditionally called the parable of the prodigal son, but it could be more appropriately called the parable of the loving Father. He is the key figure in the story, which centers on His unending, fathomless love for all His sons.

Jesus's inspiration for His parable may have come from Adam. Just as the first created man chose to abandon his Father in the ancient garden, so the prodigal left his father's home. Possibly he was driven by a desire to prove himself, though in actuality he had nothing to prove to his father. He already had his complete love and approval.

But a deep-seated need for approval lies within every man, and it often drives him to desperate extremes. While usually derived from a lack of some sort in our material lives, it finds its deeper source in Adam's need to "win back" his Father's approval after failing Him.

The prodigal's desire to find approval took him away from the one place where it could be found. His father's love allowed the prodigal son the freedom to search in far-off places. Leaving home, the son found that the farther he got away from the voice of his father's unconditional love, the stronger was the pull to a "distant country." His journey, as the story goes, eventually left him lost, lonely, loveless, and digging for food in a pigsty.

In the midst of his despair and loneliness, the prodigal son remembered: there was a father who gave him everything he asked for and, though weeping, wished him well on his journey. Remembering this, the prodigal decided to go back. It may never be the same, but at least he would be home.

Similarly, I believe that God the Father has placed within each one of us an internal photo album that is a faithful reminder of a better place. I believe that this is the original homesickness, a fundamental part of our human nature. Our collective memory tells us that our true home is in the presence of our Father—and He has left the light on, waiting for our return.

The closer the prodigal son got to home, the clearer his memories became. As he crested the hill upon which his home sat, he saw a figure in the distance. The person seemed to be peering intently in his direction. It was his father, who suddenly took off running toward him.

What the prodigal son didn't know was that his father had been waiting every day since he had left. He sat on the front porch day after day, gazing longingly into the distance, anxious for his lost boy to return. As his father reached him and pulled him into a bear hug, the son started to give the speech he had so carefully prepared: "I am no longer worthy to be called your son. Make me like one of your hired servants" (Luke 15:19, NKJV).

But his mouth was crushed into his father's shoulder as they embraced. No apologies required. No recriminations given. Just "Let's have a party!" In this masterful story are hidden great nuggets for every father, giving him wisdom in handling the struggles through which his children may walk.

But in addition to advice, there is also an invitation. The story reminds us that we all have a heavenly Father, and that no matter how far we may feel we have strayed, He is waiting for us to come home. You may have wandered far away, but you are never too far gone to turn back. He is waiting with open arms.

From there, from that place, from that position, we can begin our true journey into manhood.

THE TRANSFORMATION BEGINS

The journey to manhood and ultimately fatherhood begins with love. The importance of experiencing, love, care, and encouragement in anyone's life cannot be overstated. Max Muller, the famous German philologist, once said, "A flower cannot blossom without sunshine, and a man cannot live without love."[1]

Love and encouragement can come from different sources: parents, relatives, friends, or children. Men typically equate love and encouragement with acceptance. Sadly, our society has replaced strong, positive words that build up with sarcasm and criticism that belittle and cut down. Moreover, we now live in a world of digital dialogue where heartfelt communication is often reduced to a broken sentence, an "I luv u" text message. There is no genuine emotion or sacrifice to show that we truly care for one another. As men, we all too often do not live in a world of emotion.

> The journey to manhood and ultimately fatherhood begins with love. The importance of experiencing, love, care, and encouragement in anyone's life cannot be overstated.

I have counseled my share of men, and they typically have a difficult time expressing themselves. We are told that men who express themselves emotionally are weak. But I contend that any man who is able to express his inner feelings and hold fast to his masculine identity is a true man's man.

When was the last time you shared your heartfelt emotions

with someone you trusted? How difficult is it for you to tell your son, daughter, wife, or a close friend that you love or believe in them? It is important to note that even though it may seem that you have never experienced the kind of love and encouragement I have described, I would contend that our heavenly Father has always loved and encouraged you.

Sit back and reflect on your life. Think about the teacher, friend, or coach who encouraged you. In many instances, it may have been your wife or someone you were dating. God intentionally placed some of these people in your life to provide you with a word of encouragement just when you needed it the most.

I find myself reminding men that God is love. He openly expressed His unconditional love for His Son who, in turn, openly expressed His unfailing love for His Father. This is a perfect example for us to follow as godly men. Of all of God's commandments, Jesus said, the greatest is love.

CALL TO ACTION: GETTING TO THE PINNACLE

There is nothing of greater importance, nothing more critical to tapping into your reservoir of power, than to get into an intimate relationship with the power source—God.

This can prove challenging, spiritually, so let's address it first from the physical perspective. Is there a father or father figure in your life you look up to? Most men have someone they can think of, but the problem is that we don't always embrace the connection.

Here are some things you should do:

1. Build or reestablish the communication. Maybe you haven't talked in weeks or months. Make it a priority to talk to this person on a regular, consistent basis, maybe once a week, once a month—you decide.

2. Increase physical contact. Maybe you typically greet each other with a handshake. If so, when you're shaking hands, place your left hand on top of his. A hug may seem awkward, but we do it in sports, so why not with someone we supposedly love and care about? Do you ever put a hand on his shoulder? How about a kiss on the top of the head? Intimacy involves touch, and if we are ever to become intimate with God—to touch His heart and have Him touch ours—we must learn how to first embrace the men He has placed in our lives.

3. Do you have a picture of this man? Do you have a picture of yourself with him? If not, take one the next time you are together, and display it where you can see it often.

As we work through any issues of embracing an earthly father or father figure, we are better positioned to embrace our heavenly Father.

Chapter Four

THE PROCESS: MAINTAINING FELLOWSHIP WITH GOD

THERE ARE FOUR keys of knowledge that will help men unlock the truth and reality of the untapped power within them: purpose, peace, priority, and position. When a man comes to understand how to use these keys, then he will be able to impact and influence his family and community in the manner for which he was created.

A MAN'S PURPOSE

When you examine nature, you cannot help but be mesmerized by the intelligent design and handiwork of our Creator. He is precise and particular and does nothing without a purpose and a plan. No better place can that purpose and plan be found than in God's greatest creation, man.

When men are unsure of their purpose, the consequences of this uncertainty are far-reaching and extend way beyond just themselves, to their homes and communities. When a man does not know his purpose, he puts his family in peril. When the family is in peril, the community is at risk. When the community is at risk, the entire social order is threatened.

Away from the Maasai village, where I saw a clear sense of place, in so many communities around the world it seems many men have lost their sense of purpose. They are asking questions like these:

- "Why was I created?"

- "Why am I here?"

- "Where am I supposed to go?"

Until a man can answer these questions, he will never truly know his purpose. And until a man truly knows his purpose, he will never be able to truly unlock his untapped power and live out the fullness of his destiny. He will spend his days existing, perhaps, but not really living.

Once men understand their broader purpose, they must also realize that God has a more specific purpose for their lives based on the talents they were blessed with.

Yes, we have all been blessed with talents; some of us may have been gifted with more than others, but we are all of equal importance in God's eyes. It is critical that men identify and accept their God-given purpose to find the pathway to peace. Otherwise they will live out their lives second-guessing themselves and never feeling as if they have achieved all they were destined to.

> Once men understand their broader purpose, they must also realize that God has a more specific purpose for their lives based on the talents they were blessed with.

The only way to truly understand your purpose or "your calling" is to spend time praying, meditating, reading the Bible, and seeking guidance from other God-fearing men and women. This will strengthen your faith.

But, as I always say, after you pray, you must then do something. Faith without works is dead, we are told in James 2:17. So take your faith on a test drive by spending some time away from your day job doing what the Holy Spirit is guiding you to do. I assure you that if the Spirit is leading you, an inexplicable inner peace will rest within you. Afterward, you will want to do nothing more than to pursue what you were called to do, even if it means making less money.

Jackie Robinson was arguably the first African American to successfully play Major League Baseball. He was, by all accounts, a superb athlete, winning the Rookie of the Year award, a World Series medal, and a league MVP award and was eventually voted into the Baseball Hall of Fame.

But did you know that Branch Rickey, the general manager of the Dodgers and a devout Christian, had something else in mind for Jackie? Yes, he wanted a phenomenal ball player, but his true purpose for Jackie was to lead the effort to integrate baseball. In fact, he used to hurl racial slurs at Jackie just to see if he could handle it.

Jackie had an explosive temper that initially affected his play. However, once Rickey explained to Jackie what his ultimate purpose was, he went on to rein it in and break the color barrier. His is a great example of how the power of understanding your purpose is critical to living a full and successful life.

God has a plan for every man, and God has a purpose for every man. In Jeremiah 29:11 (MSG), we read, "I know what I'm doing; I have it all planned out—plans to take care of you, not abandon you, plans to give you the future you hope for." God created man as the foundation upon which family and social order is to be built. The solution to the world's "men problem" is to help them acknowledge and accept this starting point as God's plan and to encourage them to embrace it as their reason for existence.

There is a fascinating article in a 2014 Association for Psychological Science newsletter titled "Having a Sense of Purpose May Add Years to Your Life."[1] It states that having a sense of purpose in life may help you live longer, no matter your age. It also cites a previous study that suggested that finding a purpose in life lowers mortality above and beyond other factors that are known to predict longevity. This is fascinating because, while the information is presented as an amazing revelation, it does not actually state anything new—just read your Bible! You see, God's primary purpose for you is to know Him, and that involves studying His Word. When you study the Word you gain wisdom, and Proverbs 9:11 (NIV) says, "For through wisdom your days will be many, and years will be added to your life."

God has been telling us that for thousands of years, yet people are marveling over a recently written article that essentially says the same thing!

A MAN'S PEACE

Though they have to remain vigilant, always living with the threat from lions and other dangerous predators, the Maasai men have a quiet and sure inner peace that is unlike anything I have ever witnessed. Nothing seemed to worry them or cause them to be anxious or fearful. I don't find that same confidence and assurance among many of the men I encounter. I detect a growing unease and uncertainty about what it really means to live in each of the spheres as a modern-day man, husband, and father.

I see men who are at war rather than men who are at peace. They are at war with themselves, with others, and even at war in their homes. But to obtain peace is not merely to cease to engage in conflict or war. After all, the Maasai men have survived through conflict and danger for their entire existence, yet their peace remains. It is a peace that, I believe, all men desire. It is an inner strength of character, an inner power, of which Paul wrote in Philippians 4:7 (NKJV), "...the peace of God, which surpasses all understanding."

Some men think they can find this peace by escaping—into a world of drugs, alcohol, pornography, or illicit sexual activities. Others chase their hobbies and "boy toys" like sports and cars. Some look for it in money. This is not real peace. This is avoidance. Real peace is the acceptance and acknowledgment of who you are and why you exist as a man.

Men must stop fighting who they are and what they are supposed to do on this earth. We are desperately trying to fit in with the trends of modern society instead of being comfortable with who we are. The pathway to real peace is realizing that men were meant to be good stewards of the earth and servant leaders. Trust me, the feeling you will get from being a true servant leader will be like nothing you have ever felt before.

A MAN'S PRIORITY

Although many men are wondering why they exist, we have not been left on our own to guess or to try to figure out the answer. Proverbs 19:21 (NIV) says, "Many are the plans in a man's heart, but it is the Lord's purpose that prevails."

> The pathway to real peace is realizing that men were meant to be good stewards of the earth and servant leaders.

In other words, while there are many opinions in the world about what a man, a husband, and a father should be, there is only one that counts, only one purpose and plan that will lead to fulfillment and destiny.

From the creation story in the first three chapters of Genesis, it is in the Garden of Eden that we get our first glimpse of God's plan and priority. Before God gave Adam an assignment, a job (the Garden to tend and keep); before God gave Adam the practical task of naming every animal; and before God gave Adam a wife to love and serve, God gave Adam himself.

Genesis 2:7 (NKJV) says, "And the Lord God formed the man of the dust of the ground, and breathed into his nostrils the breath of life; and man became a living being." God gave Adam "the breath of life." He gave Adam His Spirit.

God's priority for men is that we love Him wholeheartedly, seek Him in all we do, and complete the mission or tasks He gave us. God's intent from the beginning was to have fellow-ship with both male and female, but God began with the male as He established His order. It was when man missed his quiet time with God, his daily moments of meditation and conver-sation with his Creator, that God called out to Adam saying, "Where are you?" (Gen. 3:9, NKJV).

God's priority for man is fellowship—a personal, intimate relationship. A man who understands God's desire for intimate fellowship with him, and who makes this his own priority, will be a man at peace, with an inner strength that enables him to stand up to lions and to release the untapped power within him.

A MAN'S POSITION

Having formed Adam from the dust of the ground, God set him in the place he had prepared for him, the Garden of Eden. God set the man in the context in which he was supposed to remain to fulfill his purpose and priority.

What was that environment? "Eden" comes from the Hebrew word meaning "delicate, delight, or pleasure."[2] The word for garden means "an enclosure" or "something fenced in." This was not an ordinary yard. This was the place where heaven turned into earth. God placed the man in an environ-ment that represented the glory of heaven. It was as though God prepared an incubator for His new children, the new off-spring created in His image and after His likeness.

God placed Adam in the Garden so that he could be con-tinually in His presence, enjoying intimate fellowship. Imagine, the man would have the privilege to walk and to talk with God daily. He could hear God's voice, commune with Him, and be at one with Him always. God never intended for Adam to move from the Garden. He actually intended the Garden to be replicated over the earth. God wanted Adam to take the presence of the Garden and spread it throughout the world so that God's kingdom would be on earth—as it is in heaven.

This is the meaning of the command for Adam to "Have dominion over the earth" (Gen. 1:28, NKJV). God has not changed His mind about what His vision is for the earth...nor has He changed His mind about the role and the responsibility He has given the male and the female in fulfilling His vision.

Men today are still to advance the kingdom of God throughout the entire earth. Habakkuk 2:14 (ESV) says, "For the earth will be filled with the knowledge of the glory of the Lord as the water covers the sea." This is the vision God gave the man, a vision of what the world should look like and what the world should be like under man's leadership and under man's authority. As stated in Genesis 2:15, 19–20, God delegated His authority by allowing Adam to tend and keep the Garden and to name all other creatures on the earth. Only the Creator of a thing has the legitimate authority and right to name it; God transferred that authority to Adam.

Therefore, the man who had been given the vision and the authority was also given the position of being the visionary leader—to carry out the plan of God to extend and cover the entire earth with His Garden of delight and delicate pleasure. He was given the position of being the visionary leader because God is a God of order, and He made a sovereign choice to make man the foundation, the one upon whom He would build the social order.

God created woman out of man and gave her to Adam as his helper. Not as his slave nor as his unequal partner, but as his equal partner. To complement him, not to complete or to compete! When Adam and Eve fell in sin through their disobedience, God asked Adam, not his wife, "Where are you?" (Gen. 3:9, NKJV). This was not a question of location. This was a question of position. Adam was not supposed to allow Eve to turn and go the other way. He was not supposed to allow her to discuss with the serpent what God had told him and expected him to be responsible for. It was as if God was asking these questions:

- "Why are you out of the position I placed you in?"

- "Why are you following your wife and not Me?"

- "Why did you get out of your position and lose sight of the vision for which I gave you responsibility?"

Men, it is critical for us to understand that our position is that of visionary leaders who have been given the responsibility of making God's presence known throughout the earth. God positioned us as the foundation. And He needs us, He expects us, to stay in position. This position is to be in God's presence at all times. It is not enough to simply visit a church or synagogue or some other house of worship every now and then. Like the Maasai warriors, we need to be in touch with the Creator daily, constantly, hearing His voice, listening to His commands, and following His directions.

When we fail to stay in position and make our fellowship with God our priority, we will make the same mistake Adam made. When we lose sight of the vision, we get out of position—and we lose our authority to lead our families and our communities.

The Maasai men are at peace—with themselves, with one another, with their world, and with their Creator—because they understand their priority and their position. As a result, their families are secure, and their children are obedient and respectful.

When a man is properly aligned in priority and position, the resulting peace enables him to be a powerful and impacting force in the world.

CALL TO ACTION: MAINTAINING
THE PRIORITY

Time is money, but time is also power. This is why you need to spend regular time with an all-powerful God. What man wouldn't love to spend time with his favorite sports superstar? But the question is, what can they do for you other than boost your ego and give you an autograph?

> When a man is properly aligned in priority and position, the resulting peace enables him to be a powerful and impacting force in the world.

If you are not in the habit of spending time with God other than maybe Sunday morning in church, here is where you might start:

1. Have an early-morning quiet time. Start off with five minutes and build from there. Say a prayer. Read a passage from the Bible. Then sit still, fighting your mind from racing forward into your day, and try to hear what God may be saying to you.

2. Walk your domain with God. Yes, your neighbors may think you're crazy, but daily take a walk around your house. Breathe in deeply and exhale. Thank God for His provision, and ask Him for direction for your day.

3. When you get home from work, don't be so quick to reach for the TV remote or to turn to your secular music or favorite social media. Take a few minutes to listen to one or two instrumental or worship songs. Allow God a chance to give you the peace that you so

desperately desire. Let Him speak to you concerning your evening and set the tone for your interaction with your family.

4. In the evening, go outside and stand on your porch or patio. Breathe in deeply and exhale. Thank God for getting you through another day. Ask His blessings and protection over your household for the evening.

Combined, these four suggestions may take as little as twenty minutes of your day. But as they become a regular practice, watch how the time increases and how you value your daily time in God's presence. Watch how you begin to tap into ideas, resources, plans, and goals like never before.

Chapter Five

THE PARENT: LEARNING FROM TWO SONS

- "I don't want any children."

- "I don't want children right now."

- "I don't want any more children."

- "I don't want to adopt children."

IF ANY OF these statements apply to you, you might be wondering if you can skip over this chapter. Let me assure you that the information on the following pages is essential for every man if he is serious about accessing his untapped power.

Whether you have children or not, hope to or don't plan to, you face the same question: Do you want to be fruitful?

If someone were to dig a hole with the purpose of putting you in it, you wouldn't take too kindly to the idea. If they attempted to put you in that hole, they would have a fight on their hands. And you definitely wouldn't appreciate them throwing dirt on your head.

> Whether you have children or not, hope to or don't plan to, you face the same question: Do you want to be fruitful?

To fight for your physical life is only natural, but God is also calling men to learn how to fight for their spiritual lives as well. In that fight, we are reminded of John 12:24-25 (NKJV), which says, "Most assuredly, I say to you, unless a grain of wheat falls into the ground and dies, it remains alone; but if it dies, it produces much grain. He who loves his life will lose it, and he who hates his life in this world will keep it for eternal life."

Life is constantly digging a hole for us, putting us in it, and trying to bury us alive! But remember, you are a seed. Others may have meant it for evil, but God is using these people and situations to help us become fruitful. We are that kernel of wheat, that seed. For us to become fruitful for the kingdom of God, there are fleshly patterns, attitudes, and actions that must first be buried, covered, and killed off. This calls for a commitment to self-renunciation as opposed to self-preservation.

The question is, do we truly want to be fruitful? Or do we enjoy the way we are in our flesh more than what God wants us to become in the spirit? To be successful in Christ, we can't complain about every hole that's dug for us. We can't be discouraged every time we are lowered into that hole. And we can't give up when they start shoveling dirt on our heads.

We are seeds, and this is the process that all seeds must go through before they break through the earth and become productive. Get used to being buried—it is part of the process, and you have to learn how to respond properly.

TWO SONS

I want to introduce you to two boys who are the key to your deliverance and success. They are an invaluable asset for accessing your untapped power. Whether you have or want physical children or not, trust me, you need to "adopt" these two.

In the Bible, Joseph had two sons after going through his many trials. They were symbolic of what he had to do to gain deliverance from his trials and become successful. If you don't fill out the spiritual adoption papers on these two boys and welcome them into your life, you will be cheating yourself of God's best for you.

In Genesis 42:50–52 (KJV), we read, "And unto Joseph were born two sons…. And Joseph called the name of the firstborn Manasseh: For God, said he, hath made me forget all my toil, and all my father's house. And the name of the second called he Ephraim: For God hath caused me to be fruitful in the land of my affliction."

SON NUMBER 1: MANASSEH

Joseph's first son was named Manasseh, which means to forget. He is key to your deliverance because you have to be able to forget all the toil, headaches, and painful situations of the past.

How do you adopt Manasseh as your son? How do you forget what's been done to you in the past? All while Joseph was growing up, his brothers hated him and never had anything kind to say about him. They threw him in a well and left him to die. While in the pit, Joseph probably heard his brothers talking about killing him. They took him out of the well and sold him into slavery. Later on, Joseph did time in jail for doing the right thing.

How easy is it to forget all of that? It's almost impossible. Most of us can still remember lesser evils perpetrated on us by our siblings.

In the general sense, the word "forget" means to put out of your mind. In this verse, however, the word means to remit. This is to refrain from enforcing punishment. It means to forgive a debt. So the word "forget" here has nothing to do with your memory, but everything to do with your actions! You're going to remember a whole lot of bad things that happened in your past, but the question is, are you going to act on them in a way that does not honor God and jeopardizes your future?

Or are you going to fill out the adoption papers and let Manasseh bring a fresh new start to your life? It's okay if you don't forget, but Manasseh is there to remind you not to act on what you remember. Every time you see that person, you may feel the pain of what he or she did to you. It's in those moments that you need to call on your boy, Manasseh, to help keep you from taking action that will make matters worse.

> You're going to remember a whole lot of bad things that happened in your past, but the question is, are you going to act on them in a way that does not honor God and jeopardizes your future?

We would love to have the pain of the past erased from our memories, but thank God for how He designed us. You have to touch a hot stove only once, and the memory is with you forever. Because of the pain of getting burned, most people don't play with fire again. Pain serves as a reminder to position ourselves so that it doesn't happen again.

But spiritually we continue to play with fire, and we get burned again and again. With Manasseh as your son, the painful actions of others are not necessarily erased from your memory, but the sinful reactions that can cause you further pain are erased from your things-to-do list.

SON NUMBER 2: EPHRAIM

Adopting Manasseh is the foundation to your deliverance, but deliverance is a process, and the second step involves adopting Joseph's second son, Ephraim. The name means fruitful. This son is key to your deliverance because the word "deliver" means to bring something forth or produce something. So you have to be fruitful to be delivered.

Ephraim represents fruitfulness, productivity, and prosperity, and that's a mind-set that most people don't have when they are going through major trials. But just because you are going through tough times does not excuse you from being fruitful. Verse 52 says, "God caused me to be fruitful" where? In the land of my affliction!

Most people say that when they get over this, they are going to do this, and when they reach this point, they are going to do that. That's not faith. Anybody can "do good" when things in their lives are good. God says He wants to see some fruit from your life while you are going through tough times.

Many of us are still in captivity because we don't understand what a blessing it is to have a son named Ephraim. He is adopted into your family in the land of your affliction. Not after you get out. In the land of your affliction, you must remain faithful to become fruitful to gain freedom. But the first thing so many men do in the land of their affliction is stop being faithful. They look at the situation they're in, and faith gives way to rationalizing.

We're quick to say, "God understands what I'm going through. God understands if I stop tithing for a while. God understands if I stop coming to church for a while." But we need to understand how God operates. Yes, He understands, and He may have mercy on you, but do you want just mercy, or do you want His abundant blessing as well?

I want God's mercy when I'm not doing all I should be doing, but I also want His overflowing blessing when I am doing all He asks me to do. No matter how difficult and slow the process is, I'd rather move from being faithful, to being fruitful, to gaining freedom, to walking in favor. I want to be the one God uses to have mercy on others rather than the one who is always crying, "Lord, have mercy on me!" But that doesn't happen until you make up your mind to become a father to Ephraim.

PAY THE PRICE, REAP THE BENEFIT

Most people look for the right time to have children, especially when it comes to finances. After all, children are expensive. But when it comes to what God has planned for your life, you can't afford to wait. When it comes to the damage that is being done to your self-esteem, your willpower, and your faith, it gets more expensive over time to afford Manasseh and Ephraim.

Every man needs to become a father to these two boys today. It may seem difficult, and in your flesh it is. But if you look at those verses, they say, "God hath made and…God hath caused." God does all the work! You see, you don't have to support these boys; they will support you. Just having them in your life will be a blessing you can't afford to miss. All you have to do is open up your life to the two sons of deliverance.

Joseph got his deliverance, and his dreams came true. He didn't retaliate against those who tried to bury him. He forgot about it. He didn't use his misfortune as an excuse to fail. He became productive and fruitful in the midst of his trials. How badly do you want your dreams to come true? The verse in 2 Timothy 2:12 (KJV) says, "If we suffer, we shall also reign with him: if we deny him, he also will deny us:" Don't deny the seed God has placed in you. Don't be discouraged because for that seed to come forth, something in each of us must be buried; it must first die. Don't be afraid of that death. Realize that God is bringing new life into your life, and He is doing it through the two sons of deliverance.

When you adopt Manasseh and Ephraim, you tap into the power that is necessary to help you press on in difficult times. You value your future in spite of your current situation. You envision a life of success in spite of those who have tried to bring you down. In this life you will experience some hard times, and you will have some enemies. As a man on a mission, you cannot afford to not be a parent to the two sons who hold the key to your deliverance.

> Don't deny the seed God has placed in you. Don't be discouraged because for that seed to come forth, something in each of us must be buried; it must first die. Don't be afraid of that death. Realize that God is bringing new life into your life, and He is doing it through the two sons of deliverance.

What are you waiting for? Sign those adoption papers!

CALL TO ACTION: ADOPTING THE TWO SONS OF DELIVERANCE

1. There may be people in your past who have wronged you. You may have forgiven them, but you struggle because you can't forget what they did. That's okay. It does not make you any less spiritual if you still remember. As long as you are not retaliating, you are doing fine in the eyes of God. Spend some time in prayer asking Him to reveal and remove anything in you that even hints at retaliation against others.

2. Do you have plans for what you are going to do once your situation turns around? If not, that may be part of the reason you are still in that situation. Begin the process of putting those plans into action today. Your commitment to fruitfulness in the midst of the storm is a major key to your deliverance.

3. Identify the areas in your life where you are rationalizing why you are still stuck. Remind yourself that you have no biblical grounds for remaining in that place. Tell yourself that in

addition to God's mercy, you also want His blessings, then chart out a course of action and begin to walk in faith toward God's best for your life.

Chapter Six

THE PLAN: ACCEPTING
RESPONSIBILITY

FOLLOWING THEIR CIRCUMCISION ceremony, the Maasai youngsters are sent out into the surrounding area on their own to recover. When they return, healed, they are expected to join the men in providing for and protecting their families. This crucial call to the acceptance of responsibility is passed down from generation to generation.

As he lay on his death bed, King David spoke the following words to his son, Solomon: "As for me, I am going the way of all the earth. Be strong and be courageous like a man" (1 Kings 2:2, HCSV).

Last words tend to be important. When people don't have much breath left in their body, they usually don't waste it on small talk—though the famous Irish playwright Oscar Wilde is said to have quipped, "Either those curtains go or I do."[1]

For most of us, though, last words are going to be about what matters most. They are the indelible thoughts and feelings that can change lives. And if the final words of a father to a son can be expected to be both profound and significant, how much more so when there is not just the passing of a family's patronage involved, but also the transfer of a nation's leadership.

So it is no surprise that, at the end of a rich and fulfilling life, King David had some simple but important words of counsel for his son, Solomon. Here was the "man after [God's] own heart," as the Bible calls him, leaving the kingdom of Israel to another's charge. What parting words did he say about being a strong and just king? "Be a man," David urged. But what exactly is that? What does it mean to be a man? How do you become a man? When do you know you have become a man?

Most men answer that last question erroneously because of what they have been taught by the world around them. Depending on who or what they believe, they might think they have achieved manhood when they accomplish the following:

- Reach a certain age allowing them to drive, vote, or marry.

- Have their first sexual encounter.

- Take their first drink of alcohol.

- Collect their first paycheck.

"Male maturity does not come with age," observes Dr. A. R. Bernard, Senior Pastor of the renowned Christian Cultural Center in New York City, "it comes with the acceptance of responsibility." Responsibility is the one word that truly captures the essence of manhood. It is a word that reminds me of my last conversation with my dad before he died.

George Anderson stood only 5'6" tall, but he was known throughout the Cincinnati–Northern Kentucky area as "Gypsy" for the fearless, adventurous, pioneering spirit he displayed in everything he did. He rode a Harley-Davidson motorcycle that was almost as tall as he was, and you knew when he was somewhere near because you could smell his cigar mixed with the grease and fumes. That aroma said that a rugged man was around.

As a young boy, it seemed to me that everybody knew George, or "Shorty," as his closest friends sometimes called him. However, my siblings and I never called him Dad, Daddy, Shorty, or Gypsy—to us he was just George. He was not a saint by any stretch of the imagination. Yet there was no one who loved his children, loved life, and respected God more. A staunch but nonparticipating Catholic, George was determined that his boys would get a Catholic education. My mother and George never married, but he took full responsibility for his sons and did the best he could in providing for our needs.

George taught me many lifelong lessons, though he was not always aware that I was taking notes. He instructed me, in his own way, about what it meant to be a man. With only an eighth-grade education, George was a hustler. Never one to sit still very long, he always seemed to have another job, business, or scheme to "make it." This was the genesis of my own spirit of entrepreneurship and my passion for winning in life.

One warm spring day in 1994, we were sitting in front of his thrift shop on Madison Road in Cincinnati. I had stopped by to see him before heading over to see my mother. We did not say a lot; he asked about my wife and my work. But then, suddenly, he got very serious, as if he knew he did not have much time left. As I was getting up to leave, he told me as he always did, "I love you." Then he added in a gentle but at the same time commanding tone, "Phillip, always do what you said you would do, and never quit."

Not long after, George died of a massive blood clot in his leg, subsequent to being treated for yet another asthma attack at the University of Cincinnati Medical Center. Five days later, I preached my dad's funeral. Through that eulogy, I caught his spirit of manhood, which I believe changed my world and which is my driving passion to this day. His force as a man, and a father, now lives in me. George's final words to me—"Be responsible," effectively—became the foundation upon which I have built my life as a husband, father, pastor, and community servant. I have repeated them on a number of occasions to my own sons, R. J. and Bradley.

Being responsible means becoming a man of character, courage, and conviction. It means that we keep our word, as my father reminded me, and that we own our choices and our mistakes. Responsibility requires an unwavering commitment to the truth, regardless of public opinion, personal feelings, family pressures, critics, or the cultural concessions that have been made through the years. Responsibility of this kind is weighty, for sure, but it is not a burden. It is not a bad thing or a curse. Rather than something we try to shirk, responsibility should be a blessing we seek. Responsibility is the very hallmark of being a man.

Booker T. Washington said, "Few things help an individual more than to place responsibility upon him and to let him know that you trust him."[2] More recently, "Dear Abby" newspaper columnist Abigail Van Buren wrote, "If you want your children to keep their feet on the ground, put some responsibility on their shoulders."[3]

> Rather than something we try to shirk, responsibility should be a blessing we seek. Responsibility is the very hallmark of being a man.

So what does responsibility look like? Responsible men step up, stand firm, and stay put. They don't back down from what they need to do. Instead they do what they have to do to the best of their ability, regardless of whether it is convenient or not.

According to the great British politician and historian Winston Churchill, "A man does what he must—in spite of personal consequences, in spite of obstacles and dangers and pressures—and that is the basis of all human morality."[4]

Irresponsible men, on the other hand, run away. They make excuses for themselves, and they blame other people.

It has been the same way since the beginning of time. Just consider the story of Adam and Eve. Brought into perfect creation, the first couple had everything they needed or could want—at least, until the serpent came along. He tempted Eve to reach for something that was out of bounds.

When God came walking in the Garden of Eden later, He called out, "Adam, where are you?" (Gen. 3:9). It wasn't that God did not know what had happened. He saw everything that was going on. But note that while Eve was the one who first gave in to temptation, convincing Adam to indulge along with her, God called out the man.

When God asked him, "Have you eaten from the tree of which I commanded you not to eat?" Adam attempted to pass the buck. He tried to shift the responsibility on to his mate and even back on to God Himself, "The woman whom you gave to be with me, she gave me fruit from the tree, and I ate" (Gen. 3:11–12, NASB).

Some things don't change! Ever since that time, men have been seeking to escape and shift the responsibility for their poor choices and actions onto others.

MEN: THE FOUNDATION

As I have observed, society offers many different ideas about what a man should be, but it's his Creator whose opinion and definition counts. God's purpose is the only one that matters— and it is the only one that will lead a man to fulfillment and destiny. Proverbs 19:21 (ESV) teaches us that "Many are the plans in the mind of a man, but it is the purpose of the Lord that will stand."

Author John Eldredge writes the following:

> What is a man for? If you know what something is designed to do, then you know its purpose in life. A retriever loves water, a lion loves the hunt, a hawk loves to soar. It's what they've been made for. Desire reveals design, and design reveals destiny.... Adam and all his sons after him are given an incredible mission: rule and subdue, be fruitful and multiply."[5]

The same story that reveals where God placed responsibility also helps us understand why it is so critical. God created mankind in His image and after His likeness, placing him in two physical "bodies" called male and female. Together they were to have dominion, to rule over and to influence planet Earth. Theirs was a shared commission. Yet when God created "man" the spirit both male and female, He did not do so without purpose. And in Genesis 1:27, we see the divine plan unfolding in the order in which the two expressions of God's image were created.

God is a God of order, purpose, and design. So He had a specific purpose in mind for both the male and female. And while they are equal in value before Him, they are different by design and thus in their purpose.

We often hear it said these days that "the family is the foundation of society." It is true that the family is the important, adhesive ingredient that holds communities together, but God did not start to build earthly society with a family. He began with one person—He began with a man. Note that only the man came directly from the earth: Adam was formed from the dust of the earth (Gen. 2:7). I believe this is because the man was designed by God to be the foundation of the human family. Eve was drawn from Adam's side (Gen. 2:21–22): the woman came out of the man, rather than coming from the earth, because she was designed to rest on the man—to have the male as her support.

Man was the starting point of the future families that would populate the Father's world. Man was created to be the progenitor, a creator, and an executor of the future plans of his heavenly Father.

It is important not to misunderstand here. This does not mean that men get to call all the shots and women and children simply need to fall in line. Men are not given the responsibility to have dominion over people, but over the fish of the sea, the fowl of the air, and every creeping thing on the earth.

Nowhere does God give the man dominion over other men, women, or children. The responsibility that God gives the man as it relates to other people is to be a servant leader. God is looking for tender leaders, not tyrants.

But, at the same time, God knew exactly what He was doing in the manner and order of creation. He planned everything before He began to create anything. When He started laying the foundation, He knew exactly what He wanted and what the completed picture would look like. His creation is a reflection of His thoughts and plans. When He began to build the human race, God began by laying the foundation of the man. God placed man as the foundation to support the building of humanity.

If men do not accept the responsibility of being the strong foundation, then our families, communities, societies, cultures, and our nations will continue to sink in the quicksand of injustice, greed, violence, and division. Although we have many godly, well-intentioned women, there are simply some things that a woman cannot give a boy in his journey to manhood. As awesome and inspiring, devoted and dedicated as many of the women in our world are, it yet remains that they cannot give a boy who seeks to become a man an understanding of how he must become the foundation for his family and community, because they were not designed to do so.

> If men do not accept the responsibility of being the strong foundation, then our families, communities, societies, cultures, and our nations will continue to sink in the quicksand of injustice, greed, violence, and division.

I believe that men are being called by our Creator to live responsibly, as the foundations we were intended to be. Foundations are not generally seen, except during the early stages of the building process. They are most often hidden, doing their job of upholding everything placed upon them without recognition and fanfare. The work we do as men may rarely be seen or appreciated by others, but our hidden presence in the substructures of life will build a solid future for our world.

The nineteenth-century German writer Jean Paul Richter observed, "The words that a father speaks to his children in the privacy of home are not heard by the world, but, as in whispering-galleries, they are clearly heard at the end and by posterity."

NO MORE EXCUSES

Understanding and accepting our responsibility and our identity as men established by the Creator is, I believe, the key to reestablishing order and stability in our homes, communities, nations, and our world. Whether you are a father in the natural or the spiritual sense, a husband or a single man, a business executive or a laborer, it is critical that you recognize that as a man you have been given responsibility. What are you going to do with it? How will you respond?

The major problem we face today is that men, regardless of their differences, do not have a clear understanding of the purpose and power of manhood. As a result, the average man is terribly confused about manhood in general.

As pastor, author, and speaker Crawford Loritts, Jr., notes:

> The tragedy, or the blessing, is that we tend to raise our children the way we were raised. The end result of what has been done to us is more than what has been said to us. If we grew up without a heart connection to our fathers, we'll battle a seemingly irresistible inclination to be disconnected from our children. We need God to connect our hearts to our children.[6]

Perhaps it is due to a lack of role models, or the absence of strong men in their lives, or because of cultural changes and compromises, but many men are suffering from a loss of identity and a loss of purpose. . Many young boys with absentee fathers—those who are missing either physically or emotionally—are walking in quicksand, or failing miserably in life when they should be standing on the solid foundation laid by their fathers and other men in their lives.

There are many youth who are trying to find solid footing for their lives, but they continue to sink because there is just no place where they can stand on a solid foundation. The challenge is for every man to rise up and become a strong, solid foundation. We need husbands who will stand with their wives, fathers who will stand with their children, and men in general who will be there as stabilizers in their communities.

It doesn't matter what your father was like, or the relationship you had with him—you can become a strong foundation today by becoming the man you were created to be, by understanding and accepting the measure of true manhood: responsibility.

> We need husbands who will stand with their wives, fathers who will stand with their children, and men in general who will be there as stabilizers in their communities.

CALL TO ACTION: ALIGNING WITH THE PLAN

Every man seems to have pretty much the same plan: How do I get more money and more pleasure with less responsibility? We pursue this course with a passion, not realizing that it is in direct contradiction to God's will for our lives.

God gives us the ability to get wealth so that we might help establish His kingdom. That means 'more responsibility! But getting men to take on more responsibility in the face of their current pressures is not an easy sell.

How do we address this problem? Here are some suggestions:

1. As young men—and, regrettably, in many cases as older men—we need to remove the phrase "Momma, can you...?" from our vocabulary! It should be replaced with, "Momma I already...." Let's stop looking for others, especially the women in our lives, to do what we should be doing. It's time to grow up!

2. As an employee, identify that one little thing that you can volunteer to take responsibility for that is outside of your normal responsibilities. Why? Well, do you want to be considered for promotion or not? Prove yourself worth it.

3. You may not feel led to organize a community watch in your neighborhood. But maybe you and your son could you take an hour on a Saturday morning and pick up the trash along the entrance to your subdivision? Start small. Every little bit helps.

4. If you are a mother, it may be hard, but please learn to "Just say no!" to your sons. You have to learn to love them without crippling them by doing for them what they should be doing for themselves. You're ultimately hurting rather than helping—and creating a project for the woman he will marry.

5. Pastors, you may need to stop asking men to lead and start asking them to participate. The average guy doesn't want to be a deacon, trustee, elder, Sunday school teacher, or community leader—but he will help out! If you are in a

leadership position, break it down into tasks
and make the list available to men. Brother
Johnson may not feel comfortable praying for
the sick in the hospital, but he has no problem
picking up the communion supplies from the
Christian bookstore near his house. Start small,
giving men small responsibilities, and watch
how God grows it from there.

Zechariah 4:10 says we should not despise the days of
small beginnings! Untapped power is unleashed when we get
involved with God's plan and watch how He blesses ours, as
we accept responsibility.

Chapter Seven

THE PROVIDER: MEETING
THE FAMILY NEEDS

ORIGINALLY RELEASED BACK in the 1980s, the hit song "Working for the Weekend" has since been featured in several movies and advertisements. It has become something of an anthem for many who have to drag themselves out of bed in the morning to face another day on the job. But it couldn't be more wrong in its suggestion that work's only value is in providing what you need to pay for food and a roof over your head and going out on the weekends to have a good time.

God has a different view. Something interesting happened when He placed man in the Garden to tend and keep it. God first gave man a little bit of Himself as He breathed life into him. As His Spirit was breathed into that lifeless body being held in the hands of this loving Maker, man became a living being. God then gave man a place to live. He provided a place where His plan could be worked out. God then gave man an assignment—a task, a job, a purpose. Adam was to tend, to keep, and to rule. God commanded the man to subdue the earth and to have dominion over the fish of the sea, the birds in the heavens, and every living thing that moves.

What most of us do not realize is that this awesome responsibility God gave to man was not simply an authority conferred upon him; it was deeply imbedded in him. Men, you were hard-wired to be providers for your families. From the time you come into manhood, you have had a burning desire to provide for your family. It does not matter what your social or economic status may be; there is an innate drive in men to work and provide. That is why men take it so hard when they cannot find employment and, in many instances, suffer from depression when they lose a job. Men who are gainfully employed are more confident, assertive, and joyful because they are able to give their families the things in life they deserve.

God commanded the man to take the beauty of life in the Garden, with all of its splendor and majesty, and spread it to the rest of the earth. In essence, we see that God was giving man a command to be a provider for the entire earth, and being a provider is linked to being a protector. One way a man protects his family is by providing for them.

God gave man the position of visionary leadership, with the authority to carry out His plan. Because God brought the woman out of the man, after him, he is responsible for caring for the gift the Father has given him—the woman. It stands to reason that one purpose of man is to provide for his family.

Men, we are created to be the providers of everything good, healthy, and beneficial for our children, wives, churches, and communities. Indeed, the Apostle Paul wrote that "If anyone does not provide for his relatives, and especially for members of his household, he has denied the faith and is worse than an unbeliever" (1 Tim. 5:8, NKJV). And in 2 Thessalonians 3:10 (NASB), he offers a straightforward opinion "If anyone is not willing to work, then he is not to eat."

Now, I realize that there are times when work can be a hassle or when a man loses his job through no fault of his own. Those are situations where your faith is being tested and you must trust that the Lord will guide you through it, no matter how dire it may seem. But the sweat, thorns, and thistles we now experience as we work are a consequence of Adam's disobedience in the Garden. However, work can be transformed from a curse to a blessing as we embrace the grace needed to fulfill our role in God's world. Remember, the first thing we see God doing when we are introduced to Genesis 1:1 is Him being productive: God is creating the heavens and the earth and filling them with reflections of His image and His likeness.

THREE WAYS WORK IS MEANINGFUL

Our Creator God created man to be a creator as well. There is a certain imagination, wisdom, and ability that is inherent in man that enables him to fulfill this God-given responsibility. In fact, work was given to man for three primary reasons:

1. Through his work, man is able to advance the plan and purposes of God in expanding His kingdom in the earth. So in the marketplace, you are extending the kingdom of God in some way. As you work, you can manifest the life of God to others in what you do and in the way that you do it.

2. By working, man is able to fulfill his destiny by using his natural skills and talents. Each of us was created for a unique purpose and has been given special gifts to fulfill it. There is a synergy between the fulfillment of your destiny and providing for your family.

3. Man is able to provide for his own household through his work. As man is fulfilling the Father's purposes in his life, he is also creating wealth that will provide for all of the needs of the family. There is a holy connectedness between his labor away from home and his provision for his home.

This divine strategy was all laid out before God gave man the woman. Men, God commands us to work and to provide for our families. If you are physically able and not incapacitated in some way, God expects—and your wife and children need—you to be the primary source of provision, both materially and spiritually, in the home. I am not suggesting that wives and mothers should not also work. They have gifts and abilities that God has given them that are to be shared with others, too. But I will note that it is important to understand the order of things. In Genesis, we see that God gave man work and the command to provide before He gave him a woman.

> I f you are physically able and not incapacitated in some way, God expects—and your wife and children need—you to be the primary source of provision, both materially and spiritually, in the home.

In the same way, today, before a man needs a woman, he needs work to be a productive provider for the woman he will choose. In the Genesis account, God gave the man the responsibility for being the provider of the family. I believe we have the primary responsibility to ensure that our families are provided for, through our God-honoring labor.

MORE THAN JUST MATERIAL GOODS

Providing isn't just about giving physical things. We have the opportunity to pass on important life lessons at the same time—like the one I received along with a beat-up old red Huffy bicycle.

My father could not give his kids the finest of things, but he provided the best that he could. Twelfth Street, where we lived, had a steep incline at the end where it intersected with Pendleton Street. A four-way stop sign was there to control traffic, and all the kids in the neighborhood loved to get up a head of speed, fly down the hill at full tilt, race straight through the intersection, and stop at the corner store. We called it the Twelfth Street Run.

As Christmas approached one year when I was a youngster, I begged and begged for a new bike. All the other kids on Twelfth Street had nice, shiny ones with all the extra features, while my brothers and I had to share one. All I could think of was having a new bike of my own on which to make the downhill dash. George wouldn't promise me a new bike. He simply said, "I'll see what I can do." I could hardly sleep after attending midnight Mass that Christmas Eve. Finally, I dozed off. In the morning, when I looked at the secondhand bike George had for me, I began to cry. Then I stomped and ranted, and through tears of disappointment I declared, "I don't want that bike, and I ain't gonna ride it."

It wasn't the shiny new bike I had envisioned. Instead, it looked like something George had found on one of his garbage hunts, when he would drive around the area looking for items other people had discarded that he could refashion and repurpose. He had repaired and painted an abandoned Huffy.

My complaints didn't faze him outwardly, but I could see that I had hurt him inwardly. That old, used red Huffy was the best he could do, and he had given it to me with pride. After a few days of refusing to ride the bike, George looked at me and said simply, "Phillip, that is the best I can do, son."

His words punctured my defiant bubble. I got on that bike and rode it with pride and joy—that is, until the day I dared to take the Twelfth Street Run. Rather than flying full-speed ahead through the intersection, I turned to see who was watching me so that I could show off. Taking my eyes off where I was going, I found myself tangled up around the stop-sign pole, with half my bike going through the intersection on its own.

I learned that it's no fun when your pride is hurt, and more importantly that fathers provide much more than just material things—they provide care and compassion, and lessons on how to be grateful and appreciative of the efforts of others.

Fathers can create lessons out of most everything that happens in their children's lives, even as they provide physically.

Although important, it is not enough to simply be focused on making money so that we can take care of the physical needs of our family. As we meet their physical needs, we are creating an atmosphere of security for the whole family. Part of that involves not just providing for today, but having tomorrow in mind as well. We should be actively laying up treasures for the future needs of the family. But this concern about practical things needs to be balanced with other kinds of provision. Fathers have an important role in providing identity for their children. Though this may be less tangible a goal, it is no less important.

MEETING EMOTIONAL AND SPIRITUAL NEEDS

Men need to preserve some energy from their time at work so that they can also be sensitive enough to provide for the spiritual needs of their families. We must create a spiritual atmosphere in the home so that everyone is able to experience God's presence in powerful and meaningful ways. We must be providing spiritual direction for the family that will secure spiritual foundations for their lives. To do this, to fulfill our priestly and prophetic roles, we must be actively developing our own spiritual lives.

Then there are the emotional needs that must be met. How do we do that? By being there when they need us. Providing is not just about bringing a paycheck home and setting it on the table. Some guys seem to think that their work is over once they come home; actually, it's just changed. They need to switch back to their main job as husband and father. Often, though, men allow their work outside the home to interfere with providing for their family within the home. They can end up spending more time away from home than they should, justifying their absence by reasoning that they are doing it for their wife and kids—when really what they need is less money and more time at home.

Or men can be so tired from their work that when they get home, they become emotionally absent from their family. This there-but-not-there kind of attitude creates emotional insecurity. Our wives and children need us to be there *with* them and *for* them, to offer our real presence—to listen to them, to play with them, and to talk with them. It is certainly important to constantly reassure them of our love with our words, but that love must also be expressed in our involvement in their lives. Our love is demonstrated more in our actions than in our words.

Men are also to provide by being a source of unity in their families, churches, and communities. Men are created and called by God to be the ones who hold things together and do not allow things to fall apart. With no disrespect to any of the many women who are doing all they can and know how to lead their homes because the men are physically or emotionally absent, one of the tragedies of our day is the breakdown of the family and the rise in the number of matriarch-controlled and -dominated households.

Growing up, we had to look to Mama to hold everything together. This placed a tremendous burden on her—one that she was not created to bear. And although my mother and many other mothers have borne this weight in the heat of the day, mothers were never created to carry the load of being the source of provision, identity, or unity. That role and that responsibility is meant to rest squarely on the shoulders of fathers and husbands. The man of the house is supposed to provide the stability that unites and holds everything together. The word "husband" means "house band"—he is the band that holds the house firmly in place, united and stable.

> With no disrespect to any of the many women who are doing all they can and know how to lead their homes because the men are physically or emotionally absent, one of the tragedies of our day is the breakdown of the family and the rise in the number of matriarch-controlled and -dominated households.

Men need to be crisis managers. Living together in a family can be trying and often involves conflict. Through the wisdom given them, fathers must know how to creatively resolve the conflicts that often confront their family. They must teach how to respect the space of other members of the family. They must help everyone see that they are not in the family just to be served but to serve one another. When misunderstandings happen, men do not ignore them, hoping that they will go away. They jump into the middle of the conflict and bring peaceful resolution.

> The man of the house is supposed to provide the stability that unites and holds everything together. The word "husband" means "house band"—he is the band that holds the house firmly in place, united and stable.

MORE WORKING, LESS SHIRKING

I see a growing number of men who look to avoid their responsibilities, especially as a provider, because of what I call the "loser's limp." That's what happens when a ball player tries to catch a pass but misses the ball because he misjudges things. He doesn't want anyone to know that he blew it, so he falls down and gets up limping to hide his failure. The same thing happens when a runner who is favored to win is getting beaten in a race; he comes up limping with a sudden muscle pull or cramp. This "loser's limp" is just camouflaging failure. As a pastor, I hear these excuses all the time:

- "It's the way I was raised."
- "My father left my mother."
- "It's because of this woman I have."
- "My job demands so much time."

No matter what a man's excuses may be for failing to fulfill his divine, God-given role, the fact remains that if he is not a provider, he is not getting the job done.

Author Les T. Csorba, a former White House adviser for presidential personnel, has a name for these kind of men: phantom fathers. In his book *Trust: The One Thing That Makes or Breaks a Leader*[2], he cites a story told by family expert Dr. James Dobson, whose second child arrived just as his popularity skyrocketed following the success of his book, *Dare to Discipline*.[3]

Dr. Dobson was asked to appear on talk shows, travel to promote his new book, and present "question-and-answer" forums for parents. Already a busy college professor, he was soon overwhelmed. Then he received a life-changing letter:

> My father, who always served as a beacon in dark times, saw what was happening to me and wrote a letter that was to change my life. First, he congratulated me on my success, but then warned that all the success in the world would not compensate if I failed at home. He reminded me that the spiritual welfare of our children was my most important responsibility, and that the only way to build their faith was to model it personally and then to stay on my knees in prayer. That couldn't be done if I invested every resource in my profession.

Dr. Dobson resigned from the university and developed a ministry that allowed him to stay home more often. He turned down requests to speak and began his radio program; travel was no longer an issue. He did it all to honor his relationship with his wife and children, while launching Focus on the Family, one of the most influential family ministries in the world. He discovered how to provide physically, spiritually, and emotionally. Recognizing the importance of that balance, Dr. Dobson said, "The relationship with those you love will outweigh every other good thing in your life."

CALL TO ACTION: EXPANDING YOUR ROLE AS THE PROVIDER

"I pay the bills! We have a roof over our heads, food on the table, and clothes on our backs!" If you are a man who can say this, you are to be commended. But while these are your primary duties as provider, they are not your only ones. When men see their primary duties as providers, it's understandable why they come home from work and indulge in six to eight hours of "me" time before retiring for the evening.

Men, your assignment is to develop visionary leadership for your home, which causes you to look beyond the immediate needs of the household and begin to anticipate future needs. This will require reducing your "me" time and investing some of it in meeting additional family needs.

Consider the following needs:

1. Do you have adequate insurance in the event of your death, to cover the funeral expenses? Do you have adequate insurance in the event of your death to continue providing for your family? If not, what areas do you need to cut back on to ensure the necessary coverage?

2. Do you have a will? Is it updated? Do you have additional instructions for your family to follow

in the event of your death? If not, you need to attend to these details.

3. Each individual in your household has emotional needs. You should regularly set aside some of your "me" time for some "we" time with them. It is not acceptable to come home and shut down because you had a long day. This "we" time should consist of questions like "What can I do for you?" "How can I help you?" "How was your day?" Maybe you can't do anything about the particular situation they tell you about, but just being available to listen is providing much-needed emotional support for your family.

Just providing the basics for a family is tough enough today, I know. But when you go beyond the basics and provide for your family's emotional and future needs, you tap into your power as a provider by unleashing the synergy of a united household that is primed for accomplishing great things.

Chapter Eight

THE PROMOTER: EXHIBITING TENDER STRENGTH

In American culture, football players are among the most celebrated examples of men who possess a warrior physique and fighting spirit. Physically intimidating and explosive, they are extraordinarily powerful. Watching someone who stands 6'6" and weighs 290 lbs. run a forty-yard dash in less than six seconds is impressive. It is, however, equally if not more impressive to see these men visiting hospitals and spending time nurturing the spirits of sick children.

A man's role is not merely that of protector, but also of promoter. A protector guards against evil, while a promoter ensures that good flourishes by encouraging others to become all God intends for them to be. A man's role involves walking the tightrope between being a lion and being a lamb, or being like Abraham Lincoln, whom Carl Sandburg described as "a man of steel and a man of velvet."[1]

Mind you, there is no formula or process to help you determine how much of a lion or lamb you should be at any particular time. Only the Holy Spirit can give you that true balance. It was demonstrated perfectly in the life of Jesus, who gave us the absolute pattern of holistic masculinity.

A father has the power to give his children roots and wings—roots that will stabilize and anchor their lives in God, and wings that will give them the courage to fly away from home to discover their own destiny. Fathers are the fertilizer for the soil and the wind beneath their children's wings. They nourish and encourage. They send and lead. They comfort and correct. They compel and propel.

When sons and daughters receive positive encouragement and inspiration from their fathers, they grow up well balanced and able to face life's difficulties without the pressure of trying to be perfect, of feeling the need to always fit in with "the crowd." They grow up knowing that they are unique, different, special, and capable of adding value to any situation in which they find themselves. They are inspired to greatness because they are motivated out of love to please their fathers.

> A father has the power to give his children roots and wings—roots that will stabilize and anchor their lives in God, and wings that will give them the courage to fly away from home to discover their own destiny.

When Ashley and Bradley, our two younger children who are just a year apart, went off to college, Cynthia and I became "empty nesters." But it was not long before I got a call from each of them. Ashley was concerned and a bit confused about the newfound freedom of college life. She did not feel comfortable about being there, she told me.

"Sweetheart, you are going to do fine," I assured her. "I have confidence in you, and I am sure that you will be all right." It was not long before Bradley called, too. He was homesick and felt like his life was falling apart. "Son," I told him, "it's going to be okay, and you are going to do fine. I have every bit of confidence in you." Hearing my words, suddenly everything fell into place for him. Why? What happened for both Ashley and Bradley? Their father spoke reassuring words of confidence, protecting their emotions and self-esteem.

Not only are fathers a source of inspiration for good; they are also a force that can keep their children from evil. A dear friend of mine tells of going to a party during her freshman year of college. Sometime during the evening, she decided she needed to leave because she was simply not enjoying it. When asked why, she replied, "Someone started smoking some marijuana, and people were drinking. And even though I wanted to be there and take part in what they were doing, in my mind, I kept thinking, *What would happen if my daddy walked through that door?*" When a man understands the true strength of fatherhood, he will use his power to inspire his children to greatness, and to the fulfillment of their destiny.

But it is no easy task. Many fathers who are not aware of the power they wield in their role have made the mistake of abusing it and of misusing their leadership place and influence. Instead of inspiring, protecting, and providing for their children, they end up manipulating and unreasonably controlling their sons and daughters because of their own weaknesses.

> When a man understands the true strength of fatherhood, he will use his power to inspire his children to greatness, and to the fulfillment of their destiny.

It's important to remember that children both admire and fear their father's strength. On the one hand, they want their father to be strong and powerful, in the sense of being self-confident and determined, but they may also be frightened at times by that power. Walking the careful middle ground between dominance and permissiveness can sometimes be difficult for a father. But it is this ability to travel between these two realms that increases a man's influence in his children's lives. A balance between exercising authority and granting freedom gives the child security and confidence.

When children feel accepted and respected by their father, they will begin to develop close feelings of mutual affection. Fathers who are never involved with their children, who are too permissive or too dominant, are not likely to become close to their children. Fathers who act as vigilant disciplinarians but who show no tenderness create a climate of coldness that puts distance in their relationships.

Fathers exercise great influence in the psychological development of their children. Talking about feelings has traditionally been easier for women than for men, but a good father must know how to express his love for his child. It is the power of his father's love that will provide an eternal foundation for his children.

To increase his influence, it is important for a man to spend qualitative time getting to know each of his children individually—their unique fears, aspirations, abilities, and struggles. As he understands his children uniquely, he will be able to more competently direct them in the ways of the Lord.

> Talking about feelings has traditionally been easier for women than for men, but a good father must know how to express his love for his child.

A Father Is:

There in every memory
    See his love and care
    Strength and hands to count on
    Freely he does share
    Provider, toil so faithfully
    To make our dreams come true
    Give strong and tender discipline
    Though it is hard to do
    A Father is God's chosen one
    To lead the family
    And point it to His will for life
    Of love and harmony....[2]

—SUE SKEEN

Given that a man's role is so crucial in the home, we should not be surprised that so many are absent, physically or emotionally. I believe the causes of this trend are not just cultural or financial. At their root, they are spiritual. For if the enemy wanted to thwart God's plan for humankind, what better way than to keep men from fulfilling their pivotal role? Satan knows that if he can undermine and cause division in the home, between husband and wife, and between fathers and their children, he undercuts God's plan to reveal His love in the one institution that best reflects His plan and purpose— the family.

That being the case, a man will not be able to resist these forces by willpower alone. This battle is ultimately of a spiritual nature and can be won only with spiritual power. The noted Welsh pastor and author, Dr. D. Martyn Lloyd-Jones, said it well:

> Human willpower alone is not enough. Willpower is excellent, and we should always be using it; but it is not enough. A desire to live a good life is not enough. Obviously we should all have that desire, but it will not guarantee success. So let me put it thus: Hold on to your principles of morality and ethics, use your willpower to the limit, pay great heed to every noble, uplifting desire that is in you; but realize that these things alone are not enough, that they will never bring you to the desired place. We have to realize that all our best is totally inadequate, that a spiritual battle must be fought in a spiritual manner.[3]

As men, we must understand that we are in a battle, whether we like it or not. Everyone is caught up in this spiritual war, whether they know and confess Jesus as Savior or not. Believers may be more of a target because they are at least aware of the devil's schemes. So we need to know how we are going to be attacked; how our family, community, church, and culture is going to be attacked; and how to respond to those satanic assaults.

Luke 11:21–22 (AMP) says, "When the strong man, fully armed, [from his courtyard] guards his own house, his belongings [goods] are undisturbed and secure. But when someone stronger than he attacks and overpowers him, he robs him of all his whole armor on which he had relied and divides his [goods as] spoil."

For men to rise to their greatest potential, they must understand that there is another world that is not seen—a world of the spirit. In that world are great forces that are either contributing to the fulfillment of the Father's plan in this world or working against that plan. The evil side must be understood and fought against. Where does a man get the necessary tools and instruction to fight this spiritual battle in a secular world that does not believe in a spiritual world? He must turn to the Father. His Word can give us all we need to fight and win.

Men have a tremendous responsibility for their families— far greater than I first realized when I got married more than forty years ago. But the more I have studied the scriptures, the more I have come to realize how much the Word of God says about our responsibilities as fathers. Fulfilling this responsibility requires recognizing that whatever a man allows to come into his home will have either have a positive or negative effect on his wife and children. As fathers, we must be very sensitive to this so the environment of our home is conducive to raising children who love God and who desire to follow Him.

In Mark 3:27 (NKJV), Jesus says, "No one can enter a strong man's house and plunder his goods, unless he first binds the strong man." We can apply this verse to how Satan attacks the family. To come in and destroy a man's goods as well as his wife, children, and community, Satan first has to attack and bind the father, the *strong man*, and then go after the others. If Satan can keep the father from fulfilling his role, and if he can restrain the father from protecting his family, he will gain access to the whole family.

The good news is that a Christian man has access to God's power and authority, through the name of Jesus Christ, to protect his wife and family physically, socially, and spiritually. This ability is not to be found in this world. It comes from a higher place, a heavenly source. It comes from a man's heavenly Father, who enables him to physically stand between his family and any possible physical harm. Socially, he can absorb the pressures of situations that may be awkward or compromising and not allow his family to go unprotected. Spiritually, he can stand between his family and the powers of darkness in this world and the rulers of spiritual wickedness in heavenly places.

TAPPING INTO THE SOURCE OF SPIRITUAL POWER

To access this power, a man must develop a real relationship with God. It is not enough to have a surface knowledge of Him, or a passing acquaintance. To survive the kind of satanic attack that will come against him, he must be willing to dive deeper. He must learn to open his spirit and soul to God. If he does, he will discover a new source of power and authority flowing into his spirit that will then empower his soul.

Through this intimate, dependent relationship with the Father, a man can discover new abilities and new gifts to help him meet his calling to be priest, prophet, and protector in his home. These spiritual gifts and abilities are critical to the fulfillment of his roles. There will be times when he will not have the human wisdom or power he needs to protect his family. But as he lives in God's presence, he will find the authority to stand for his family against any attack of the enemy.

When a man recognizes his authority, so does the enemy! A man who is surrendered to the lordship of Jesus Christ will, by his very presence, create a protective environment in his home.

The authority of this unseen spiritual protection—emotionally, mentally, materially, spiritually, or otherwise—will repel anything that is not the will of God. A godly man will protect that which is true. In an age of so many lies and half-truths, this will require great spiritual discernment, a measure of knowing and understanding that is possible only as he opens himself to the voice of God.

Promoting the truth means that a man will stand against that which is not true when it attempts to invade his home—through music, the Internet, other sources of modern technology, or other people. In the Bible, Satan is called the father of lies. A godly man's spiritual antenna will always be up and functioning, detecting any lie that seeks access to his home. He is the ultimate truth detector.

> Promoting the truth means that a man will stand against that which is not true when it attempts to invade his home—through music, the Internet, other sources of modern technology, or other people.

That role may take him beyond the walls of his home, like the father who noticed changes in the attitude of his elementary school-age daughter. She was no longer interested in going to church and to Sunday School, seemingly as a result of the influence of one of her teachers at school, a forceful agnostic. The father decided to take charge of this negative situation and went to the school to sit in on his daughter's classes. Wanting to put him on the spot, the agnostic teacher instructed the man's daughter to go outside and look up into the sky.

When the young girl came back, the teacher asked, "Did you see the sky?"

"Yes."

"Did you see the sunshine?"

"Yes."

"Did you see the clouds?"

"Yes."

"Did you see God?"

"No."

"Well," the teacher replied, "there you have it—God does not exist!"

The classroom was silent for a moment as the young girl looked back at her father. She was confused and needed reassurance. Her father stood up and asked to share a thought with the class. After being given permission, he asked all the children to look around the classroom. He asked them, "Do you see the blackboards?"

"Yes."

"Do you see any books?"

"Yes."

"Do you see the flag?"

"Yes."

"Do you see the teacher's desk?"

"Yes."

By now, the children were getting tired of the questions, but the father pressed on.

"Do you see your teacher?"

"Yes."

"Do you see her brains?"

"No."

"There you have it," the father said. "Your teacher has no brains!"

A man who understands his position in Christ will step out when he needs to. He will exercise his authority to bind and to loose. That means he can protect his sons and daughters from philosophies and mental attitudes that may cause serious emotional traumas later on in life, by promoting what is right. True protection shields the family, protects the community, defends the church, and guards nations against the onslaught of Satan.

It means standing against the pollution of pornography, the

abomination of abortion, and the cancer of racism and classism. Unless men step up to exercise their God-given spiritual authority to resist and cast down the evil wave of atrocities, I fear that we will see more lives destroyed in the years to come than we ever have before.

Men, not on our watch! We are to be like God's ultimate security guards for our society. When the men show up, everyone in the family, the community, or the church should feel protected. To serve in this way effectively, you must acknowledge that you are in a real war. So either you prepare to fight or have your destiny, hope, and blessings taken from you by your enemy. There is no place for timidity and passivity on the battlefield. You, your family, and your community are on one, be sure of that. Forces of evil are seeking to destroy you and yours.

War is a vicious, all-out encounter with the enemy. War is not just waiting around and letting the enemy bring the battle to you. Instead, you take the battle to the enemy by learning how to go on the offensive.

CALL TO ACTION: DEVELOPING IN YOUR ROLE AS THE PROMOTER

We're familiar with the stern, serious father-figure type. He doesn't say much, but when he does, he means it, and you'd better be listening. We still need him. But we also need him to be multidimensional; the health of his family depends on it. It is imperative that the same voice that barks commands also breathes soft counsel.

Men, take note of your conversations with your wife and your children. Listen to yourself. Is there balance in your message? Are you guilty of just bellowing out the marching orders for the day, or do you also speak life, hope, and purpose into those you love?

We may think, "If they just do what I say, everything will

be fine!" But the truth is, if they just do what you say, they feel like they are nothing more than servants.

When a man taps into the power of the promoter, he launches his family and enables them to hope, dream, and achieve far more than what's on his things to-do-list. For this to happen, he must first make time to listen to them—not to correct them or judge them, but to show support for them. You may consider what they are pursuing to be a total waste of time, but resist the urge to say it. They are fragile, and squashing their dream today may discourage them from ever dreaming again. It is not important that they get it right the first time. After all, did you?

> When a man taps into the power of the promoter, he launches his family and enables them to hope, dream, and achieve far more than what's on his things to-do-list.

Let them figure it out on their own. But be there for them as the promoter, the encourager your family needs, and they, too, will learn of the untapped potential within themselves.

Chapter Nine

THE PLAY: MOVING TO THE BALL

OKAY, GUYS, ITS halftime. We've covered a lot of ground, but the game isn't over. Let's bring it in, huddle up, and discuss how we prepare for the second half. 'Using an example most men can relate to—football—let's look at how we can reach our untapped power with the synergy of teamwork. Christianity is best played on offense, where we control the ball. But over time, many of us have repeatedly fumbled the ball over to the enemy. So we now have to move to the ball and stop the enemy. Then we can return to playing offense instead of always reacting defensively to everything.

Moving to the ball simply means getting involved in the action to help your team be successful. Never assume someone else is going to make the play; all of us should be moving to the ball. Good football players pursue the ball until the whistle blows. As Christians, we're not listening for a whistle, but for the final trumpet that will announce the return of Jesus. Men, we are to be continually moving to the ball. That means getting to the place where we're best able to make an impact for God.

Hebrews 10:25 (KJV) urges, "Not forsaking the assembling of ourselves together, as the manner of some is; but exhorting one another: and so much the more, as ye see the day approaching."

This is a call to position ourselves regularly to confront the enemy. When we all gather at church on Sunday, Wednesday, and other days, we're moving to the ball. We're getting to the place where we can, as a team, make an impact for the glory of God. Football players regularly huddle together and encourage each other. And as they see the opposition approaching a score, they exhort each other more. Our praise and worship is an intimidating fight song to the enemy. Our prayers are seen by the enemy as an unfair advantage, as we get to talk to the Head Referee. The Bible is our playbook, full of plays that the enemy can't stop. This is why we should be excited about moving toward the ball.

Hebrews 10:23–24 (KJV) says, "Let us hold fast the profession of our faith without wavering; (for he is faithful that promised). And let us consider one another to provoke unto love and to good works."

Have you ever seen football players celebrating, giving high fives and congratulating each other after they have moved to the ball and stopped the runner? They're making a statement. They're holding fast to a profession they made to win. They're provoking each other, "showing some love, " and encouraging each other that what they just did, they will do again and again. Moving to the ball then becomes exciting because you can sense the victory.

When we sense the victory, we'll move to the ball in prayer, praise, worship, serving, Bible study, and witnessing. We won't assume that someone more talented than us is always going to be there to make the play. It takes the entire team moving to the ball to ensure that our defense is as strong as it can be. When we overly rely on our "star players"—the pastor, elders, and deacons—we become weak.

WHY SHOULD WE MOVE TO THE BALL?

Consider this example. A young man goes to church and decides to turn from a life of drugs. We're excited he joined, but nobody moves to the ball by calling him, encouraging him, or making time for him. He took the first step, but we fail to move to the ball. The ball represents a scoring opportunity. When we fumble an opportunity and fail to move to the ball, Satan will! Meanwhile, we sit around wondering why there are not more men in church.

> When we sense the victory, we'll move to the ball in prayer, praise, worship, serving, Bible study, and witnessing.

Matthew 12:43–45 (KJV) gives us some insight into what's happening in situations like this: "When the unclean spirit is gone out of a man, he walketh through dry places, seeking rest, and findeth none. Then he saith, 'I will return into my house from whence I came out'; and when he is come, he findeth it empty, swept, and garnished. Then goeth he, and taketh with himself seven other spirits more wicked than himself, and they enter in and dwell there: and the last state of that man is worse than the first. Even so shall it be also unto this wicked generation."

IS YOUR ASSIGNMENT KEEPING YOU FROM YOUR GOAL?

Each player on defense has an assignment to cover a specific area of the field or to cover a particular player. The problem we run into is that we often let our assignment get in the way of our goal.

Your assignment may have you on the other side of the field, but once the enemy commits to a certain play, your goal now is to move to the ball. It doesn't matter what your assignment is, once that runner crosses the line of scrimmage or once that ball is in the air. Your assignment just changed. It's time to move to the ball.

We all have different life assignments that keep us busy and on the go. But once Satan crosses the line and tries to advance his position, you must forget your assignment for a time and move to the ball.

Your assignment may be to go to work, but if your sister in Christ just got into a serious car accident, then you take time off work and go to the hospital. You move to the ball! Your assignment may be to enjoy a quiet evening with your family, but if your brother in Christ is stranded because of car trouble, you go help him. You move to the ball!

Satan is trying to advance the ball and score to discourage those who are facing difficulties. Just because he is not running at you this time is no excuse for not moving to the ball. Every church member is a part of our team. And when we don't move to the ball, we weaken our defense.

In Luke 14:16–20 (KJV), we read, "Then said he unto him, 'A certain man made a great supper, and bade many: And sent his servant at supper time to say to them that were bidden, Come; for all things are now ready.' And they all with one consent began to make excuse. The first said unto him, 'I have bought a piece of ground, and I must needs go and see it: I pray thee have me excused.' And another said, 'I have bought five yoke of oxen, and I go to prove them: I pray thee have me excused.' And another said, 'I have married a wife, and therefore I cannot come.'"

In this passage, "the man," who represents God, fixed a great supper and invited people to come, but everybody made excuses. In the same way, Jesus has prepared great things for us, and He's calling us to come.

But we may offer one or more of the three excuses to be found in the story. The first is the investment of our time and money to the extent that we're entangled. The second excuse is our entanglement with our jobs. The third excuse is our entanglement with personal relationships:

- "I know the pastor called a meeting, but there are things I need to do."

- "I need to get some things ready for work."

- "I have to take care of some family business."

None of these are bad things, but when they consistently keep us from responding and moving to the ball, the church will struggle to be successful in her mission. We must have faith to believe that when we move to the ball, God will move in our own circumstances, too.

When a defensive back decides to blitz, leaving the man he is supposed to be guarding so he can go after the quarterback, his assigned opponent is wide open to catch a pass. But he knows that if he quickly moves to the ball, he will sack the quarterback before he gets a chance to throw the ball.

> We must have faith to believe that when we move to the ball, God will move in our own circumstances, too.

There is always some risk involved in moving to the ball when you have another assignment. This is why faith is required—faith in your teammates to cover for you, faith that your defensive coordinator is calling the right play. Moving to the ball takes faith to believe that your assignment is ever-changing and that, as you adjust, God will send someone else to cover for you.

In 2 Timothy 2:4 (KJV), we read, "No man that warreth entangleth himself with the affairs of this life; that he may please him who hath chosen him to be a soldier."

As team players, we can't become so intent on our individual assignments that we're out of touch with our team goals. In football terms, we have to learn how to shed our blocks. If nobody knows how to do this, we end up with a lot of solo tackles. That means it's one-on-one and if that one defender slips or misses the tackle, the other team scores because nobody else is moving to the ball to help.

THE REWARD OF GANG TACKLING

We don't need a lot of solo tackling. Ecclesiastes 4:9–10 (KJV) says, "Two are better than one; because they have a good reward for their labour. For if they fall, the one will lift up his fellow: but woe to him that is alone when he falleth; for he hath not another to help him up."

The good reward for at least two people moving to the ball is that one player can hit the opponent low, and the other player can hit him high. The low man gets the legs, to stop the runner from going forward. That allows the other man to hit him high and hopefully knock the ball loose. If the ball is being thrown, one man can prepare to make the tackle, and the other can go for the interception. But if you have only one person moving to the ball, that player has to be very careful and cautious because he has no help. When you play conservatively, you get only tackles, but all the while the other team is steadily moving the ball down the field for a score.

It doesn't matter how many tackles you make if you still lose the game. Many games are decided by turnovers. How many times did we take the ball from the enemy and go the other way for a score?

Two are better than one because they have a good reward for their labor. Have you noticed how football players help each other up when they fall? You may not move to the ball in time to make the tackle, but you get there anyway to check on your teammate. I may be running a little late, but I still cared enough about the team to show up!

CHAMPIONSHIP TEAMS HUSTLE

David, the writer of Psalm 119, says in verse 60 (KJV), "I made haste, and delayed not to keep thy commandments."

Why are we often so slow getting to the ball? Why are

we late for church and slow to give our time and resources? There should be no delay in doing what God has called us to do. Championship teams hustle. Churches of excellence have people outside lined up to get in. They love what they do. They come early for pregame warmups to get loose. They're excited. They can't wait to praise and worship and hear the Word preached by the coach. They quickly move to the ball. That's what makes them champions.

KEEP YOUR EYE ON THE BALL

One reason we're slow getting to the ball is because we're quick to follow the wrong thing. The enemy runs a reverse, and we get faked out and end up chasing the wrong man. We're in a hurry to leave church because we're busy chasing leisure, our things-to-do list, dreams, and careers.

Psalm 16:4 (KJV) says, "Their sorrows shall be multiplied that hasten after another god: their drink offerings of blood will I not offer, nor take up their names into my lips."

Meanwhile, we're quickly pursuing the wrong ball, thinking it will make us happy, constantly trying to figure out why we're so sad. But when we keep our eye on the ball, our sorrows won't be multiplied because we won't get faked out.

In Psalm 119:37 (KJV), David asks of God, "Turn away mine eyes from beholding vanity; and quicken thou me in thy way."

We have to keep our eyes on the ball if we're going to move to it successfully. It's hard to be tricked by the enemy when our eyes are on the Lord instead of on man. Wisdom teaches us not to follow man because he doesn't know where he's going. The world is in trouble because the church doesn't see the reverse that the enemy is running. David said, "Quicken thou me in thy way." In other words, "Help me see the ball clearly so I can move to it."

I don't know about you, but I want to be as quick to move

toward God as I can. I don't want to chase the wrong thing in vain and find out that I'm still not happy.

REROUTING THE ENEMY

Ephesians 4:27 (KJV) says, "Neither give place to the devil."

When we all move to the ball, we don't give place to the devil. He has no place to run. We cut off all his avenues of escape. This doesn't happen when only a few of us are pursuing—we all need to be in hot pursuit. That's how we win. When we stay out of church and don't get involved with the team effort, we provide the enemy with a scoring opportunity.

Have you ever wondered why some people go through the same issues and problems over and over again? When we don't move to the ball, Satan can run the same play over and over. Until we move to the ball and stop the play, Satan has no incentive to run a different one. He will ram that same play right down our throats because we are not responding in the right way to stop him. When men move to the ball, we reroute the enemy until he is cornered and stopped. He then is forced to scratch his head and regroup.

One benefit of men moving to the ball is that the enemy begins to anticipate it. Before he does anything, he knows we're going to respond in number. He understands that when he picks a fight with one, he has to face ten others. So the enemy becomes more careful not to pick on one of us because he anticipates group retaliation. He second-guesses himself every time he even thinks about messing with one of us. He abandons his game plan and flees.

SUPPORTING YOUR KEY PLAYERS

When we don't move to the ball, key players get weary. When a player feels he's the only one contributing, he gets frustrated and tries to do too much, and it's only a matter of time before he's injured, retires, or asks to be traded.

The prophet Elijah reached that point. In 1 Kings 19:10

(KJV), it says, "And he said, I have been very jealous for the Lord God of hosts: for the children of Israel have forsaken thy covenant, thrown down thine altars, and slain thy prophets with the sword; and I, even I only, am left; and they seek my life, to take it away."

Elijah got upset because he felt that the rest of God's people weren't moving to the ball. He said, "I'm tired of being the only one out here making plays." So he retired and went to heaven. But in 1 Kings 19:18, God told Elijah, "You weren't the only one. I had seven thousand others."

Yes, there were others, but because they weren't moving to the ball, Elijah felt he was all alone. Men, moving to the ball is not a luxury; it's a necessity if we are to be successful in our mission. When we play as a team, the enemy can't pick us apart one by one. The untapped power of a man materializes not only when we lead, but when we show up in numbers to support and assist.

CALL TO ACTION: MOVING TO THE BALL

1. In your church, identify some of the men who are the key players, the ones making a lot of solo tackles. Call, e-mail, or text them and let them know you are ready to start moving to the ball. Ask how you can assist and support them.

2. Identify the entanglements that have kept you from moving to the ball. God is not cutting anyone from the team, but you have to be able to shed a block sometimes! As part of the team, can you make a commitment to Bible study, men's fellowship, a prayer meeting, and a service project at least once a quarter?

3. Sunday morning is pep-rally time. Reflecting on Hebrews 10:25, we seem to be good at assembling, but what about exhorting? Small talk is

fine, but who are you speaking to and building up with your words? What other man is going to be encouraged to move to the ball because of your words? Exhort at least one man each Sunday. Exhort at least one man during the week.

4. Listen for opportunities to move to the ball. When someone says he has bought a house and is moving, or when someone says he is finishing his basement or working on his car, this is an opportunity. It's not about your physical ability or skill set, but when you display a willingness to support others, it builds the bonds on the team. It increases the likelihood of moving to the ball being reciprocated and/or duplicated.

5. Championship teams hustle! Is it your norm to be "fashionably late" to church and other meetings? If so, commit to correcting this by showing up a few minutes early.

> The untapped power of a man materializes not only when we lead, but when we show up in numbers to support and assist.

Chapter Ten

THE PROTECTOR: RELEASING
THE WARRIOR SPIRIT

A UNIFORM AND A badge may make someone look like a security guard, but it takes more than that to deter serious criminals. Once they have decided on a potential heist, thieves do some serious research to find out just how well those on guard duty perform their functions. Are they focused, diligent, and well trained, or are they lazy and overweight, sitting around eating fast food and passing the time?

Just as these criminals develop well-thought-out plans to steal our physical possessions, the devil and his evil spirits do the same to steal our souls. To the unbeliever, this may sound fanciful; however, I assure you that this is serious spiritual warfare. Every moment of the day, the devil is doing battle with us, trying to influence our thoughts and emotions to get us to turn away from God.

There can be little doubt that we are losing the battle. Money, gang violence, drugs, pornography, homosexuality, and premarital sex are just a few of the weapons Satan is using to turn men away from God. Satan knows how to use the latest technology: just check out the hate-filled comments on some of the social media sites. Think about the types of shows that are aired on TV or the Internet, the songs played on the radio, or the news that is reported, and it becomes painfully clear that we are in a fight for our spiritual lives.

Men, I will be as clear as I possibly can: we are in a spiritual battle and, like Adam, we have been appointed as security guards for our gardens. The question is, how well are we going to fulfill that role? What do we need to learn? How do we need to train?

To protect our families and communities effectively, we must develop a warrior's spirit. As protectors, we have to be willing to risk all that we have, including our own lives, if necessary, to protect those given to our care.

That is going to require courage. Some people misunderstand bravery; they think that it means being fearless. I disagree; having no qualms in the face of danger can just mean that you have underestimated the situation! When the enemy attacks, it's natural to want to retreat, to duck and hit the ground, looking for cover. It isn't wrong to seek shelter for a while: the harsh realities of living in a world of evil will stun even the strongest.

> To protect our families and communities effectively, we must develop a warrior's spirit. As protectors, we have to be willing to risk all that we have, including our own lives, if necessary, to protect those given to our care.

But a man of courage will rise up and stand to protect himself and his family, he will engage the enemy despite his concerns. Any good soldier knows that the longer he just lies there and does nothing, the greater the likelihood is that he will become a casualty. If he just goes home and sits in a corner, turns out the lights and pouts, or gets into bed and pulls the sheets up over his head, moping, complaining, whining, and hoping the battle will go away, he will be destroyed.

Sooner or later, a soldier must get up and fight, or die. As you do, remember this: Jesus came to earth, died on the cross of Calvary, and rose again. He gave you all His authority, gifts, wisdom, strength, and the power to use His Name. He shed His precious blood to defeat death, hell, and the grave, ascending to heaven, where He made an open show of Satan and rendered his power null and void. Then He sat down at the right hand of the Father to be your intercessor and your mediator of every good gift.

He did not do all those things for you to be intimidated and defeated. He did all of this so that you can enter into His victory. 1 John 3:8 (NASB) says of Jesus, "The Son of God appeared for this purpose, to destroy the works of the devil." Do not be deceived: Satan has no feelings of sympathy toward you. If you do not resist the devil, he will not flee from you—but he will come to "steal, kill, and destroy" (John 10:10, NASB) and continually devastate you and your family.

God wants you and your loved ones to thrive, to live in abundance, prosperity, and health. He wants you to be a blessing to your family. But if you shrink back in the heat of the battle, you will never make it; you will miss out on what God has promised you, and your family will suffer.

Have you ever wondered why so many families are weak and defeated, suffering in poverty and lack, with no confidence or joy, and no life-giving relationships with one another? It is because they are attempting to fight a spiritual war against Satan and his army of evil spirit beings with their natural minds, talents, emotions, and will.

THE WAYS OF A WARRIOR

What is the answer? We need men like those great men of God in the Bible who had the spirit of a warrior: Abraham, Moses, Joshua, Caleb, David, Peter, Paul, and many others. The warrior spirit requires a shielding, defending attitude. It means disciplined, assertive, and sometimes aggressive action. It protects your family at all costs. A man with a warrior spirit will not turn and run from a just cause. He will not flee from the devil and his schemes. If Satan raises the stakes, the man with a warrior spirit will call his bluff.

I saw this attitude in the Maasai. They did not go looking for trouble, but they were ready for it should it come their way.

They did not brandish their weapons to make themselves look tough, like the would-be tough guys who wave guns in some rap videos. But it was clear from how the Maasai handled their spears and knives that they knew how to use them and would not hesitate to do so if necessary.

> A man with a warrior spirit will not turn and run from a just cause. He will not flee from the devil and his schemes. If Satan raises the stakes, the man with a warrior spirit will call his bluff.

Like the Maasai who would never be without some form of protection close at hand, warriors dress for battle every day. Daily they rise and put on the whole armor of God. They dress for battle. According to Ephesians 6:14-17 (NKJV), "Stand therefore, having girded your waist with truth, having put on the breastplate of righteousness, and having shod your feet with the preparation of the gospel of peace; above all, taking the shield of faith with which you will be able to quench all the fiery darts of the wicked one. And take the helmet of salvation, and the sword of the Spirit, which is the word of God."

In doing so, they are protected from head to toe and equipped with all they need to take the fight to the enemy. The one area that is not covered in this spiritual armory, you may notice, is the back, and there are two reasons. First, it means that you should never, ever turn your back on the devil. If you do, you are giving him an opportunity to wound you in an unprotected area. So don't turn around. Never walk away and say, "I've had enough." Never do a 180 and say, "I can't take this anymore." If success is a ladder, you cannot climb it with your hands in your pockets. Second, it takes willpower and determination to resist the enemy head-on. Mahatma Gandhi said that "strength does not come from physical capability but from an indomitable will."[1] Dr. Martin Luther King, Jr., put it this way, "Our lives begin to end the day we become silent about things that matter."[2]

It takes courageous determination not to turn from the conflict. But when the battle gets tough, always remember that you are not in the war by yourself—for while you may not wear armor there, God has your back.

He is even more concerned about the protection of your family than you are. You are not alone. There is One who is there for you. In the words of John Henry Cardinal Newman, the nineteenth-century English church leader:

> He has not made us for naught; He has brought us thus far, in order to bring us further, in order to bring us on to the end. He will never leave us nor forsake us; so that we may boldly say, "The Lord is my Helper; I will not fear what flesh can do unto me." We "may cast all our care upon Him who careth for us." What is it to us how our future path lies, if it be but His path? What is it to us whither it leads us, so that in the end it leads to Him? What is it to us what He puts upon us, so that He enables us to undergo it with a pure conscience, a true heart, not desiring anything of this world in comparison of Him? What is it to us what terror befalls us, if He be but a hand to protect and strengthen us?[3]

As he admonishes us to dress for battle in his letter to the Ephesians, the Apostle Paul reminds us that the conflict is really taking place in the heavenly realms, not here on earth—though its effects may be evidenced in our lives. The enemy is launching missiles (thoughts) at our minds, hurling fiery darts (arrows of distraction) at our lives, and doing anything he can to get us to lose our hope and our faith in God.

In 2 Corinthians 10:3-4 (NKJV), Paul writes, "For though we walk in the flesh, we do not war according to the flesh. For the weapons of our warfare are not carnal but mighty in God for pulling down strongholds."

PRAYING IN FAITH

One of our greatest resources is prayer. Recognizing that we are engaged in a spiritual battle means acknowledging that there's more to life than what we see. So we must seek the will and the ways of God, to be sure that we are following His plans and purposes and not just trying to get God to validate our little, finite plans.

I believe that we should pray protection over our families, but I am not suggesting that men should pray to be able to avoid trouble. Instead, we need to pray that we will be courageous and able to walk through our troubles. As Phillips Brooks, sometimes called the greatest American preacher of the nineteenth century, said, "Do not pray for easy lives. Pray to be stronger men! Do not pray for tasks equal to your powers. Pray for power equal to your tasks."[4]

At the National Hispanic Prayer Breakfast in 2002, President George W. Bush emphasized the need for prayer when he said the following:

> Throughout our history, Americans of faith have always turned to prayer—for wisdom, prayer for resolve, prayers for compassion and strength, prayers for commitment to justice and for a spirit of forgiveness. Since America's founding, prayer has reassured us that the hand of God is guiding the affairs of this nation. We have never asserted a special claim on His favor, yet we've always believed in God's presence in our lives. Prayer has comforted people in grief. Prayer has served as a unifying factor.[5]

If prayer is our fuel, then faith may be the pipeline through which it must flow. As you and your family are praying, it is critical that you understand that unless you are holding on to your faith, which Romans 12:3 tells us is God-given, then the enemy will eventually wear you down. In due course, he will cause you to give in and give up. He will cause you to surrender your faith and thus lose out on the possibility of pleasing God and being rewarded with the blessings that rightly belong to you.

That is why Ephesians 6:16 instructs us to pick up "the shield of faith," and through its proper use deflect, quench, douse, and reject any and all of the enemy's fiery arrows and darts—the distractions that are designed to destroy your faith in God, yourself, and your family. You must know how to apply true faith to your family life, challenges, and circumstances. Understand that biblical faith is not wishful thinking. It is not crossing your fingers and hoping that things will all work out in the end. Biblical faith is the confidence, the assurance, the invisible certainty that lets you know that the thing you expect or hope for is guaranteed and is going to happen.

IT'S NEVER TOO LATE TO FIGHT BACK

Now, I suspect that while all this may sound encouraging and inspiring to many, others may feel it is too late. If only they had known this sooner before too much damage had been done, injuries were sustained, and families plundered. If this is your story, let me encourage you to seek and stir up the same kind of warrior faith that David showed.

> Biblical faith is the confidence, the assurance, the invisible certainty that lets you know that the thing you expect or hope for is guaranteed and is going to happen.

You see, there was a time when he lost his family to the enemy. In 1 Samuel 30, we read about how David and his men returned to their camp at Ziklag from a campaign in the land of the Philistines. To their dismay, they discovered that while they were away, their enemies, the Amalekites, had raided the camp and robbed them of everything—including their families and possessions.

The Amalekites had stolen those families just like Satan may have stolen people and things of great value from you. After he regrouped and regained his composure, David did exactly what a man of faith should do: he prayed and asked God for direction and for a specific word (1 Sam. 30:7). Similarly, once you have surveyed the situation and recovered some balance, the first step in using your faith to fight for your family is to seek a specific word from the Lord.

Your actions cannot be based on your emotions or the need to get even with someone. There is no other base upon which you can rest your faith except the word of God. It doesn't matter how low you get, how difficult the trial, or how troubling the situation you and your family may be going through right now. It doesn't matter who rejects or slanders you, what has collapsed around you, or what has been stolen from you—God can and will speak a word to you. He will encourage you and strengthen you deep within your heart with a word, a promise just for you—if you will simply go to Him in prayer and sincerely seek His will and not your own.

> Your actions cannot be based on your emotions or the need to get even with someone. There is no other base upon which you can rest your faith except the word of God.

Next, you must act in faith based on what God has said for your family. Look at what David did in 1 Samuel 30:6-17—he acted in faith. He believed that God would do what He said He would do. God told David to go and attack and take back everything that had been stolen. So David and the men with him immediately acted on the Word of God. Prayer should always be followed by action because it is in prayer that we discover our answers and our courage. Faith always acts on the Word of God. Faith does not hear a word and then walk the other way. Faith acts on what God says and then responds.

One of the reasons so many families are in such disarray today is because we are acting on the wrong information. We're acting on what the news media, economists, and negative prognosticators say. We're acting on what the no-vision, low-vision person says rather than on what God says. Your family is in danger as long as you are governing your life and theirs based on what others have to say—rather than on a word from the Lord God Almighty, Maker of heaven and earth.

David and his men acted on the word of God and overtook the enemy, and for a solid day and night, they whipped them up one side and down the other. In the same way, God reminds us of His ability on our behalf: "Now to Him who is able to do exceedingly abundantly above all that we ask or think, according to the power that works in us" (Eph. 6:20, NKJV).

In 1 Samuel 30: 18–20, we see that God not only gave David and his men back their wives, children, and possessions; He also gave them all the possessions of the enemy. They went home with more than they had lost!

TIME TO TAKE A STAND

There comes a point in every man's' life when he must decide what he is going to do and who he is going to be. If you are going to fight to save your family and use your faith to take back what belongs to you, you must determine that you are going to get up, stand up, and show up for the fight.

There comes a time when you have to "take up the whole armor of God, that you may be able to withstand in the evil day, and having done all, to stand" (Eph. 6:13, NKJV). At some stage, you have to stand and tell the devil, "No more!"

> If you are going to fight to save your family and use your faith to take back what belongs to you, you must determine that you are going to get up, stand up, and show up for the fight.

If you are at that place, join me in the following prayer of commitment:

No more—I am not going to sit here and feel sorry for myself. No more—I am not going to sit here and let you take my wife. I am not going to sit here and let you take my children, my finances, my health, my peace, my joy, my career, my mother, my brothers, and my sisters.

No more—I am not going to let you take my calling to teach, my calling to worship, my potential, my passion, my gifts, and my talents given to me by my God!

No more, Satan. You are going to give back my family, my property, and my stuff. I come against you in the Name of Jesus Christ, and I plead the blood of Jesus against you and resist you in the Name of Jesus Christ my Lord!

CALL TO ACTION: EXTENDING YOUR ROLE AS THE PROTECTOR

We have dogs, guns, and alarm systems to assist us in our role as protectors and to help keep us safe physically. We are armed with prayer and faith to assist us in spiritual warfare. Yet there are two additional areas in which we need to stir up our warrior spirit and go into attack mode. These are the areas of debt and health, which potentially are bigger threats than criminals and demons combined.

You would fight to the death against someone breaking into

your home to harm your family. You also need to develop a plan to fight just as hard to protect your family against the intruder of debt that seeks to destroy your family. Develop also a plan involving exercise and healthy eating to fight against potential health issues that could take you out and leave your family exposed.

By taking these actions to extend your role as the protector, you will become healthier physically and financially. Think of the power you can tap into when both your body and your bank account are stronger and fitter.

Chapter Eleven

THE PRODUCER:
GETTING RESULTS

PRODUCERS ARE PEOPLE who make or cause something to happen. They are in the game, not on the sidelines watching. Producers are doers, not talkers; they get things done. They have a sense of purpose. If it's a new idea, they will see it materialize. If it's a problem, they will find a way to fix it. Producers are the ones driving innovation and creativity, and implementing change, as opposed to just managing the status quo.

Man was commanded to be a producer from the very beginning. In Genesis, we read how Adam was told to subdue the earth, name the animals, tend the Garden, be fruitful, and multiply. Why? To increase, to reproduce, and to cause the advancement of God's kingdom.

The instructions given to Adam were not so detailed that all he had to do was check a few boxes. God intentionally gave Adam the freedom to be creative within the confines of His will—you have to be pretty creative and innovative to name all of the animals of the earth! And, by the way, subduing them— which means controlling them—was no small feat, either. It took quite a bit of ingenuity to accomplish that with what was available in the Garden.

God is the ultimate producer. As Creator of the universe, He is the ultimate innovator. Scientists describe the earth as an intelligently-designed ecosystem capable of supporting itself indefinitely. God literally supplied all of our needs when He created the world. If you stop for a moment and think about how God created the universe, it is evident that He is the manifestation of divine spatial ability, which is foundational to creativity.

Spatial ability is defined as the capacity to understand and remember the spatial relations among objects. Having spatial ability is critical for certain fields of study—for instance, mathematics, engineering, meteorology, and architecture. To do his job effectively, an astronomer must be able to visualize the structure of the solar system and the motions of the objects in it.

According to an article in *Psychological Science,* "A gift for spatial reasoning—the kind that may inspire an imaginative child to dismantle a clock or the family refrigerator—may be a greater predictor of future creativity or innovation than math or verbal skills."[1] For every little boy who tinkers with an old clock or piece of machinery, there is a future producer using his God-given ability. Simply put, it is imbedded in our spirit and drives us to be agents of growth, innovation, and change. We are hard-wired to be producers.

Do you see fruit from your labors as you look at your life? Can you measure some level of progress, impact, or effect? If not, you may need to reassess what and how you are doing things. Are you working and producing as if you were doing it for the Lord?

There are a number of examples of godly producers in the Bible. In Genesis 12:1-3, God declares that He will bless your family so that your family might be a blessing to others. This is not a given, however. Just as a garden needs to be tilled, sown, weeded, tended, and harvested, so you must work the ground you have been given.

God cannot and will not act contrary to His Word. Nor will He act contrary to His laws. When you and your family are out of line with the known will of God and the revealed Word of God, He is not being cruel or harsh, nor acting against His nature, when He allows the natural consequences of your choices to come to pass. It's simply the law of sowing and reaping. All this means that being a producer as a man of God takes true faith and a great deal of effort. It requires decisiveness, determination, deliberate action, and discipline.

THE MASQUERADE: PROCRASTINATORS POSING AS PRODUCERS

This may be a touchy topic for some men, but it is critical that we address it to unlock another door to the untapped power that is within you. There is an infectious, spirit-killing disease that is spreading among men faster than any other disease in the history of mankind.

> Being a producer as a man of God takes true faith and a great deal of effort. It requires decision, determination, deliberate action, and discipline.

It can be devastating for those who allow it to spread through their minds and souls. I have seen it destroy dreams, stall careers, wreck marriages, and literally end lives. The official name of this disease is procrastination. Other names used to describe this dreaded malady are laziness, selfishness, self-pity, and ignorance. The spiritual name? "Little faith."

To find a cure for any disease, an extensive amount of research has to be done. That is followed by testing, and then clinical trials. If all works out well, the cure is administered to those who are affected.

We must approach procrastination the same way, but the good news is that the research has been done, the antidote has been tested, and the cure is readily available!

First we must understand what procrastination really is. Wikipedia defines it like this:

Procrastination is the avoidance of doing a task which needs to be accomplished. It is the practice of doing more pleasurable things in place of less pleasurable ones, or carrying out less urgent tasks instead of more urgent ones, thus putting off impending tasks to a later time. Sometimes, procrastination takes place until the "last minute" before a deadline. People may procrastinate personal issues (raising a stressful issue with a partner), health issues (seeing a doctor or dentist), home care issues (patching a leak in a roof), or academic/work obligations (completing a report). Procrastination can lead to feelings of guilt, inadequacy, depression and self-doubt.[2]

In an Associated Press article on mental health, University of Calgary professor Piers Steel was quoted as saying that "overall, more than a quarter of Americans say they procrastinate. Men are worse than women (about 54 out of 100 chronic procrastinators are men), and the young are more likely to procrastinate than the old."[3]

To be clear, there isn't a person living who does not put off something that he or she hates to do or doesn't feel like doing at some time. But with the proliferation of distractions such as access to 24/7 media programming and interactive video games, procrastination has multiplied dramatically. Millions are now feeling the effects of the latter stage of this disease: hopelessness.

Before we examine the spiritual impact procrastination has on your life, let's consider the physical and psychological consequences. Two leading experts on procrastination—Joseph Ferrari, Associate Professor of Psychology at DePaul University in Chicago, and Timothy Pychyl, Associate Professor of Psychology at Carleton University in Ottawa, Canada—noted the following:

Procrastination represents a profound problem of self-regulation. It predicts higher levels of consumption of alcohol among those people who drink. Procrastinators drink more than they intend to—a manifestation of generalized problems in self-regulation. That is over and above the effect of avoidant coping styles that underlie procrastination and lead to disengagement via substance abuse. Procrastinators tell lies to themselves, such as, "I'll feel more like doing this tomorrow." Or "I work best under pressure." But in fact they do not get the urge the next day or work best under pressure. In addition, they protect their sense of self by saying, "This isn't important."

Another big lie procrastinators indulge is that time pressure makes them more creative. Unfortunately, they do not turn out to be more creative; they only feel that way. They squander their resources. Procrastinators actively look for distractions, particularly ones that don't take a lot of commitment on their part. Checking e-mail is almost perfect for this purpose. They distract themselves as a way of regulating their emotions such as fear of failure.

The authors go on to say that there is "more than one flavor of procrastination. "People procrastinate for different reasons," they say, identifying three basic types of procrastinators:

1. Arousal types, or thrill-seekers, who wait to the last minute for the euphoric rush

2. Avoiders, who may be avoiding a fear of failure or even a fear of success, but in either case are very concerned with what others think of them; they would rather have others think they lack effort than ability.

3. Decisional procrastinators, who cannot make a decision. Not making a decision absolves

procrastinators of responsibility for the outcome of events.

The authors also added these observations:

> There are big costs to procrastination. Health is one. Just over the course of a single academic term, procrastinating college students had such evidence of compromised immune systems as more colds and flu and more gastrointestinal problems. And they had insomnia. In addition, procrastination has a high cost to others as well as oneself; it shifts the burden of responsibility onto others, who become resentful. Procrastination destroys teamwork in the workplace and private relationships.[4]

The spiritual impact of procrastination is even more devastating. It is one of the most effective ways you can prevent yourself from gaining the knowledge, wisdom, and understanding God wants you to have to live a full and fruitful life.

As an example, how often do you find reasons not to pick up your Bible and study it? How many times have you said to yourself that you were going to participate in an outreach ministry, but always found a great excuse not to?

- "I am too tired, and the weekends are my only time to relax."

- "I promised the guys that we were going to get together today; I'll do it next week."

- "My in-laws are in town."

If we are honest, probably the number one excuse for a lot of men is, "I can't do it today because the game is coming on."

The spiritual impact of procrastination is even more devastating. It is one of the most effective ways you can prevent yourself from gaining the knowledge, wisdom, and understanding God wants you to have to live a full and fruitful life.

I wonder how we would feel if Jesus gave us excuses for not having the time to answer our prayers, instead of the absolute promise that He will answer them no matter when or where they are offered, or the condition we are in at the time we pray?

IT'S TIME TO MAKE A DECISION

If a quick review of your life causes you to acknowledge that you are not seeing and producing the kind of results you believe God has in mind, it is never too late to make a change. You can start today. But where and how? As Mark O'Connell wrote, "If there are no universal recipes, no quick-fix formulas for parents and fathers; if answers, such as they are, are as much based on who one *is* as they are on what one *does*, then what in heaven's name must a man do if he is to become a better, indeed, a good father?"[5]

We may have failed up to this point, but because of His mercy and grace, God will forgive us and give us another chance to grow strong families and build healthy relationships. However, we must do our part and diligently obey Him. Part of that involves no longer allowing the media to define us, to tell us how bad, hopeless, and dysfunctional we are. As Christians, we must focus and feed on what God says about us. In Romans 12:2 (NKJV), the Apostle Paul urges, "Do not be conformed to this world, but be transformed by the renewing of your mind." We have to rearrange the way we think.

For instance, according to Ephesians 1:5, we have been adopted into God's family. Well, His family is not dysfunctional! God's family is complete, whole, blessed, and anointed with the power to change the world. Start believing it and living based on this truth, and see what begins to happen.

IT'S TIME TO TAKE ACTION

Today, more than ever, we need men of courage and conviction. Our children, churches, and communities need men who can and will make decisions and stick by them. No turning back when things start to get difficult, or flip-flopping when they become unpopular. That sort of single focus can be found and held only by men who have made some very basic decisions about who they are, where they are going, and what they are going to do.

Your actions flow from who you are in your core being. The decisions you make for you and your family will be founded on your inner, deep-down self. If you simply try to make better decisions and act better without changing your inside, there will always be a struggle; you will be trying to build a new house without first ensuring that you have a solid foundation. Jesus taught about the dangers of building a house on a vulnerable foundation (Matt. 7:24–27).

This may mean you have some internal work to do. If you have insecurities, unforgiveness, unresolved conflict, guilt, or shame, your decision-making powers will be affected. Your perspective will be clouded and your resolution weakened. But as you give yourself to the changing power of the Holy Spirit, allowing your mind and spirit to be healed and reshaped, God's transforming power will liberate you to become who you need to be and to do what you need to do. You truly start to become a man when the interior "you" has been healed and is controlled by the Spirit of God.

To make Spirit-filled decisions, you must acknowledge and address the inner child and "put away childish things" (1 Cor. 13:11, NKJV). Becoming a man is not simply a matter of getting older or growing bigger biceps. We live in a culture that puts too much focus on the exterior body; we are bombarded by commercials, movies, and billboards that promote this kind of false advertising. As a result, too many Christian men are being conditioned by culture to define themselves according to the world's standards rather than according to the Word of God.

Sadly, many men lose their ability to communicate during childhood, and it affects them negatively for the rest of their lives. They may have been silenced by abuse, neglect, ridicule, or overprotectiveness. They were never allowed to express themselves; no wonder they do not know how to now. Their inner child did not grow up; they are still affected by the little boy who was silenced and never learned to speak up and speak out.

If a man does not know how to express himself, he is restricted in his decision-making ability. Self-expression is key to decision making, and when it is impeded in earlier years, it will have adverse effects later on. Developing the ability to reason and think through issues is a lifetime process, and we often have to overcome the earlier consequences of our childhood.

Now, consider Jesus. When He was young and went missing after his family had gone to Jerusalem, Luke 2:46 (NASB) notes that "after three days they found him in the temple, sitting in the midst of the teachers, both listening to them and asking them questions." He could sit among men and interact with them. His voice was being developed right there in the middle of those religious leaders.

You may be young only once, but you can be immature for a lifetime. What is normal for a child can be deadly for a man who still understands as a child. If your understanding does not mature, your ability to make decisions will remain stunted. Paradigms and mind-sets established in our earlier years can be hard to overcome in our adult years. But mature men are able to transcend and rise above those childish mind-sets and recreate new paradigms for a new world. The signs of mature thinking are evident in men who are able to reflect, imagine, and search out truth, and then process issues and problems. They can push aside emotions and insecurities and work through the problem as they seek a determined resolution.

IT'S TIME TO BE DISCIPLINED

So how do we put away childish things and become a man? There is a sense in which we need to bring those childish parts of us to God for healing and renewal. Jesus said, "Suffer the little children to come unto me, and forbid them not: for of such is the kingdom of God" (Mark 10:14, KJV). Consider the emotions you often observe in children—anger, jealousy, fear, timidity, and passivity. How frequently are these seen in your life as a man? What are you doing about this?

> The signs of mature thinking are evident in men who are able to reflect, imagine, and search out truth, and then process issues and problems. They can push aside emotions and insecurities and work through the problem as they seek a determined resolution.

In addition to taking a serious self-assessment, we also need to challenge the world's standards and definitions of manhood and acknowledge God's plan and pattern. That will require a steadfast commitment to rejecting accepted cultural messages and refusing to swallow the lies anymore. This kind of growth is neither cheap nor easy. It will cost you because you must die to your old self. To experience a new birth, you must "put on the new self, created after the likeness of God in true righteousness and holiness" (Eph. 4:24, ESV).

You will also need to learn how to celebrate your masculinity—not an easy thing to do in a world where manhood is viewed with such suspicion. You will need to become proud to be "a man after [God's] own heart" (Acts 13:22, NKJV).

A real man realizes that his strength comes from knowing his God:

> David said moreover, The LORD that delivered me out of the paw of the lion, and out of the paw of the bear, he will deliver me out of the hand of this Philistine. And Saul said unto David, "Go, and the LORD be with thee." And Saul armed David with his armor, and he put a helmet of brass upon his head; also he armed him with a coat of mail. And David girded his sword upon his armor, and he assayed to go; for he had not proved it. And David said unto Saul, "I cannot go with these; for I have not proved them." And David put them off him. And he took his staff in his hand, and chose him five smooth stones out of the brook, and put them in a shepherd's bag which he had, even in a scrip; and his sling was in his hand: and he drew near to the Philistine (1 Sam. 17:37–40, KJV).

IT'S TIME TO BE DECISIVE

Too many men today have lost the will and the wherewithal to lead. Either because they just don't know what to do, or because they don't want to offend anyone, they avoid being definite about anything. This is a very different scenario to the one we found in Joshua 24. The man whom God had used to lead the nation of Israel into the Promised Land was by now well advanced in years. But he wanted to give the people one last word of warning before he died. So he gathered the nation and reviewed and reflected on the goodness and the faithfulness of God toward them.

Then Joshua brought the people to a point of commitment and told them to make a choice—to decide once and for all whom they would serve. Joshua was not asking for a temporary commitment; he wanted a total, complete, definite decision to follow the ways of God. Joshua set the pace by declaring his position: "But as for me and my house, we will serve the Lord" (Josh. 24:15, NASB). In doing so, he showed us the value of a man who is decisive and the difference he can make in his home, church, and community.

First, Joshua was decisive in his leadership. One of the saddest sights in the world is a man who has no courage to be the leader in his home. God created the man and gave him the honored and privileged position of leadership, and because it is an assignment from God, he is accountable to Him for how he leads his family.

Although leadership is not something you can *demand*; it is something you can *command* by your godly lifestyle and by your tender treatment of your wife and children. Too many men want to demand respect and leadership in their homes rather than be servant-leaders. The problem is that your family may comply, but they may never be committed to your leadership.

Joshua was the respected leader of his home. His family respected his decisions because they had seen his faithfulness and witnessed his dependability over the years. They had seen his consistent lifestyle; therefore, they gave him the respect he was due.

> Although leadership is not something you can demand; it is something you can command by your godly lifestyle and by your tender treatment of your wife and children.

Secondly, Joshua made a decision to be consistent. Men, we have been given the privilege of leading and giving direction in our homes, but if we are not walking what we talk—if we are living a trashy and inconsistent lifestyle, with cursing, drinking, smoking, lying, pornography, and other vices—we can never be the steady role model our families need us to be.

So many young people today look to the world of sports and entertainment for their heroes and role models because they are not finding them at home! We need more men to offer true examples by living consistent, godly lives. As you model consistency in every area of your life, you will demonstrate that God our Father is consistent and that He can be depended on.

Finally, Joshua was decisive about being a public witness to the goodness of God. Men, it is time to go public with our faith and to begin sharing with others our testimony of the love and the grace of God in our lives. We have far too many "stealth saints" who want to be Christians on Sunday yet never have a word to say about their relationship with Jesus Christ during the rest of the week. We have too many "secret agent" believers who claim to be Christians privately but are not willing to live for Him publicly. Many of our children are ashamed of their faith because they have never heard their fathers bear witness to their faith in a public fashion. Joshua made a decision to go public. He told all the people—the young and the old, the rich and the poor, the concerned and the unconcerned—that he and his household loved God and that they were going to serve Him.

If you are not willing to go into world and publicly declare your allegiance to the Lord God of Heaven and Earth, you will have a difficult time motivating your children to be totally committed to their faith in Christ. God is looking for decisive men, bold husbands, courageous fathers who will be witnesses unto Him. God is looking for men who are willing to stand and, having done all, still stand against the gates of hell and the powers of darkness.

In doing so, they will help take back our homes, streets, schools, and the minds and hearts of our wives and children. Now, *that* is producing results!

CALL TO ACTION: REDEEMING THE TIME AS A PRODUCER

A producer takes what is given him and makes the best of it. Many men are good at talking about the inequalities they face, their lack of opportunities, and other things that keep them from producing. But often our biggest hindrance is the disregard for one commodity that all men have in equal supply— time. Twenty-four hours in a day. That's all any of us have, regardless of our race, income, or education level.

Few things are going to keep you from getting the results you desire more than mismanaging your time. On average, we'll spend seventeen hours a day on work and sleep. The producer you are to become will depend on what you do with the other seven hours left in your day.

Take a full week and chart your activity, accounting for every hour that you are not sleeping or working. God gives you sleep so you can sustain. God gives you a job so you can maintain. God gives you those additional hours so you can attain. Exactly what are you attaining in them? A lower golf score? A larger belly? It may come as no surprise that a large portion of our bank of discretionary time is devoted to watching TV— watching other people tell us their vision. But what about your vision? Why be content to watch others produce when God has called you to be a producer?

Make a plan to redeem a portion of your "extra" time. Use it to plan, develop, study for, and pursue your dreams. As you tap into this bank of hours, you will discover purpose, fulfillment, and destiny.

Chapter Twelve

THE PROFESSOR: BECOMING
THE MASTER-TEACHER

GETTING THROUGH COLLEGE was a formidable challenge for me. I managed to graduate with a degree in business, but only having gained some battle scars along the way. So I don't lightly suggest that as men, we need to become professors in our homes and communities. I know it may sound too big a mountain for some to climb. Still, that is exactly we need to do and become.

As men, one of our many roles is to teach our children and those under our influence the will and the ways of God. Men must take studying the Word of God seriously and continuously learn the life messages embedded in the Bible. Unfortunately, many spend more time watching TV or attending sports events than reading the Word. I have found this to be the case even with those who profess to be true men of God. Consequently, the family structure in our country is weak, and the church has lost its influence.

But why do we need to be professors? Because professors are master-teachers, the best of the best. Why should we aspire to be anything less when there is so much at stake?

How do we become professors? The simple answer is study and teach. In 2 Timothy 2:15 (KJV), we read, "Study to show thyself approved unto God, a workman who needeth not be ashamed, rightly dividing the word of truth." Deuteronomy 11:18–19 (NIV) says, "Fix these words of mine in your hearts and minds.... Teach them to your children, talking about them when you sit at home and when you walk along the road, when you lie down and when you get up."

Once again, the primary issue that stands in the way of our tapping into our power is how we use our time. Studying and teaching will require us to spend much more time in the Word of God.

Professors who are considered leaders in their field of study are constantly examining new and existing data and developing hypotheses that provoke change or challenge the existing way of thinking. Their primary goal is to get the very best out of their students. Think about this with your biblical hat on, and you will quickly realize that Jesus was and is our ultimate professor. Yes, He is the Word that became flesh, but He also studied the Word—not because He did not know it, but to confirm how the people of that time understood and practiced the law. Using the law as His foundation, he combined His research and divine knowledge to deliver messages that challenged and fundamentally changed people's way of thinking about their relationship with God.

TO BE THE BEST, YOU LEARN FROM THE BEST

Job 36:22 (RSV) says, "Behold, God is exalted in His power; who is a teacher like Him?" God is the ultimate master-teacher; *the* Professor! So as we strive to be the best, we must learn from the best. It is not enough simply to be saved; we must heed to the words of the master-teacher.

Matthew 28:19–20 (KJV) says, "Go ye therefore, and teach all nations, baptizing them in the name of the Father, and of the Son, and of the Holy Ghost: teaching them to observe all things whatsoever I have commanded you: and, lo, I am with you always, even unto the end of the world. Amen."

One of the most important lessons that Jesus wants us to learn is that we, too, must become teachers. It's not an option; it's a command! This is not just a matter of burying our heads in the Bible and then trying to impress people with what we've learned.

Men, it is time to take increasing amounts of responsibility in rightly dividing the Word of truth. Your other talents are vital and essential, but they must become secondary to your expertise in the Word of God. We must set excellence as our goal and strive to become the professors, the master-teachers who address the issues confronting our society. Your pastor and Sunday School teachers can't do it all. You may not have or want a pulpit or a classroom, but you must become a teacher and, at a minimum but most importantly, teach your family.

> One of the most important lessons that Jesus wants us to learn is that we, too, must become teachers. It's not an option; it's a command!

What lessons can we glean from Jesus, the master-teacher, that will assist us in becoming the professor? Let's look at five things that are true of the master-teacher.

1. A MASTER-TEACHER HAS MORE THAN A SURFACE-LEVEL KNOWLEDGE OF THE MATERIAL

Colossians 3:16 (KJV) says, "Let the word of Christ dwell in you richly in all wisdom, teaching and admonishing one another...."

Attending Sunday School and then listening to your pastor preach is a great start. But it is just that—a start. Those two things alone are not going to be enough to allow the Word of God to dwell in you richly. This will require you to give up some time during the week to delve into the Word of God; that's when it begins to dwell in you richly. But the verse in Colossians doesn't stop there. It says "in all wisdom." Knowledge and understanding come from reading and studying. Wisdom comes from application. As we study, learn, teach, and then apply the Word of God, we equip ourselves to become more like our master-teacher, Jesus.

2. A MASTER-TEACHER DEVELOPS OTHERS TO TEACH

In 2 Timothy 2:2 (KJV), the Bible says, "And the things that you have heard from me among many witnesses, commit these to faithful men who will be able to teach others also."

Men, you can't do it all, and you're not supposed to. Don't put that weight on your shoulders. It's all about finding people who have a teachable spirit so that they can, in turn, teach others. Identify other men to mentor. Once we begin to learn the Word of God and apply it to our lives, we will see change. We have to be careful not to let that change puff us up with pride and competitiveness.

I've seen it too many times when men in church take the position, "I am the most learned person in this church. I teach all the classes. If there is a biblical question, I am the final authority." When you come across that way, other men are more than happy to let you reign as the professor while they focus on money, sports, and toys. We must encourage other men to get involved and become teachers.

> Once we begin to learn the Word of God and apply it to our lives, we will see change. We have to be careful not to let that change puff us up with pride and competitiveness.

3. A MASTER-TEACHER IS OBSERVANT AND FLEXIBLE ENOUGH TO RECOGNIZE TEACHABLE MOMENTS

When we say "professor," it is so easy to visualize someone with glasses standing behind a lectern in a classroom, speaking in a monotone voice about things that are way over our head. We may also envision this person having no social life, simply going from his study to his classroom and from his classroom back to his study.

That wasn't who Jesus was, and neither does that have to be you.

- Jesus taught in the mountains (Matt. 5:1–2).
- Jesus taught in the synagogue (Matt. 13:54).
- Jesus taught by the seaside (Mark 4:1).
- Jesus taught in the villages (Mark 6:6).
- Jesus taught in a boat (Luke 5:3).
- Jesus taught in the streets (Luke 13:26).

When you get the Word dwelling in you, your life becomes a lesson to others wherever you are! A master-teacher can adjust to external conditions without letting them affect his ability to get his message across. Wherever you are, you can teach.

People can look at you on the job and learn how to work with others. People can look at you playing sports and learn how to control their temper. People can look at you in a buffet line and learn about moderation. People can look at you during your worst trial and learn how to wait on the Lord, how to have peace in the midst of the storm, how to be hurt without hurting others.

People should be able to learn from us any time, any place, as we teach them by our actions and words.

Do you realize that any time you interact with people, you are teaching them something more about yourself and the God you serve? When people say, "I know you like a book," they are basically saying, "I've been around you long enough for you to have shown me just how you are going to respond in this situation." Our job as master-teachers is to make sure the book they know us by is the Bible.

4. A MASTER-TEACHER USES METHODS AND TECHNIQUES HIS AUDIENCE CAN EASILY RELATE TO

Jesus taught by parables, and it was effective. He told stories about farming, fishing, the weather, and every other imaginable subject. Your mastery of scripture is not so you can impress people by quoting chapter and verse; that is why the scribes and the Pharisees did not have the success that Jesus did. Your mastery of scripture is to show others how to relate it to everyday life.

Didn't you find those teachers in school who had no personality to be annoying? They may have known their material, but they couldn't relate to you, and they didn't try to. They just spoke in a dry tone, gave you the information, and told you the test was next Wednesday. Nobody remembers those kind of teachers in a favorable light! Nobody intentionally signs up for their courses.

Not only can doctrine and theory by itself be dry and boring, it can be overwhelming. So you use creative methods and techniques—not to excite, not to win the Most Popular Teacher contest, not to get emotions charged up, but to stimulate thinking, self-evaluation, and positive action.

5. A MASTER-TEACHER TEACHES WITH AUTHORITY

Regarding Jesus, Matthew 7:29 (KJV) says, "He taught them as one having authority, and not as the scribes."

The word "authority" means power. It means competency and mastery. Competency equates to what you know. Mastery equates to what you have lived and experienced. A master-teacher has both.

People could *respect* the teaching of Jesus. The scribes taught dull, dry legalism. They taught with intimidation and contempt. They taught out of hypocrisy, and the people didn't want any part of that. A teacher who has no authority has no respect, and a teacher who has no respect has no authority in the eyes of his student.

Think about how students used to treat substitute teachers

when you were in school. We knew they didn't have authority, so we gave them no respect, right? But can you remember some teachers who commanded your respect without having to say a word? They could just look at you in a certain way, and you would straighten up. But, then, do you also remember those who yelled and screamed and threatened you, but they still got no respect?

When you begin to learn your Bible and become competent in handling it, when you start to master it by living it and experiencing it, you will be amazed at the people who will say of you, "He is powerful; he talks about the Lord with such authority. You can just sense that he and God are very close. You can bank on his teachings." You gain the respect of people only when you as a teacher first become a student of the doctrine that you are teaching. This is what Jesus did. This is what we must do.

Competency by itself is not enough; you need mastery as well. The equation looks like this:

COMPETENCY + MASTERY = AUTHORITY

The scribes and the Pharisees in the Bible knew their stuff, but they had not mastered it. They were not living it themselves. Jesus says of them in Matthew 23:4 (KJV), "They tie up heavy, cumbersome loads and put them on other people's shoulders, but they themselves are not willing to lift a finger to move them."

It's similar in much of the church today, sadly. It is considered good to become competent in the Bible, but nobody is seeking to master it. That's because mastery takes sacrifice. Mastery means that while everyone else is trying to keep up with the Joneses, buying all the latest fashions and gadgets, you are trying to become a tither and are investing more of your money in the kingdom.

Mastery means that while everyone else is going back into the buffet line for the fourth time, you stop at two because you are working on self-control. Mastery means that while everyone else is turning in early and sleeping late, you are burning the midnight oil and rising before daybreak, doing those things that are necessary for a person who is responding to the high calling. Mastery means sacrifice when the world around you is screaming "Indulge!"

Are you content with a Bible GED, or are you working on your master's degree?

As Christians, we have the best teacher who has ever lived. And He has left us the textbook! He has canceled tests for us. He has postponed tests for us. He has gotten us through tests we were flunking. He has graded on a very merciful curve for us. He has interceded to the principal on our behalf. In return, He asks us to apply ourselves and become master-teachers in His image.

CALL TO ACTION: BECOMING THE PROFESSOR

After completing high school or college, reading is not a high priority on most men's list—except perhaps for the sports section, the funnies, and the TV guide.

What we fail to realize, however, is that the challenges we face require us to be lifelong learners. In many cases, the untapped power of a man is in unread books. We need to address this.

Here are some steps you can take:

1. Even if it's only for five minutes to begin with, read your Bible daily. Your Bible knowledge is crucial to discerning and weighing what you may read in other books and publications.

2. Don't limit yourself. It is senseless, sinful even, to know more about the statistics of your favorite team than you do about your home team—your family. The Internet is full of free

articles on parenting, marriage, dating, and every other subject you can imagine. Make sure it comes from a reputable source that is in alignment with your beliefs, but then dig in and learn what you can to improve your life and the lives of those around you.

3. How many books did you read last year? Set a goal of reading a minimum of four books a year on topics that impact your life; that's just one book per quarter. Books on sports and hobbies, and comic books, don't count!

4. Each year, identify one book to read pertaining to your employment that can better qualify you for that promotion you think you deserve.

5. Commit to a regularly scheduled class. Get involved in a Bible study. Attend Sunday School if your church has one. Check with your local community college for free classes.

Chapter Thirteen

THE PRIEST: LEADING IN GODLY FEAR

TYPICALLY, BECOMING A priest requires years of study in college and seminary, along with a considerable amount of relevant experience. That's perhaps what crossed your mind when you read the title of this chapter. Don't worry; I am not saying you have to follow that route, necessarily.

But I do believe that men have been preordained to be the priests of their households, just as in the very beginning God gave Adam a distinct leadership role in the Garden.

It is apparent to me that God intended for men in particular to teach, pray for, and provide spiritual guidance to those within his sphere of influence...in effect, to be priests. They are to act like an ordained priest who is responsible for, among other things, reading and teaching the Word of God, advising or counseling people in accordance with biblical principles, and praying for others.

In addition, I believe a priest serves as a moral compass for those around him, regardless of their relationship to him. What is a moral compass? It is having an inner sense that distinguishes what is right from what is wrong, functioning as a guide—like a needle on a compass—for morally appropriate behavior.

Men must understand that to truly embrace their role as priest, they must have a deep, personal relationship with God. A priest will inevitably face adversity because he is not afraid to stand up for what is right, regardless of what the world believes. How do men stand against powerful worldly influences? The answer is not complicated: they must fear the Lord and not man. They must stand on their convictions to serve God, regardless of how others view him.

> It is apparent to me that God intended for men in particular to teach, pray for, and provide spiritual guidance to those within his sphere of influence...in effect, to be priests.

PRIESTS MUST FEAR THE LORD

Some people call the current generation the "No Fear" generation. Certainly, it's a declaration you can see everywhere, from tattoos to T-shirts to bumper stickers. People want, even need, others to know that they are not scared of anyone or anything, and they will go to great lengths to prove it. Just look at some of the extreme videos posted on the Internet. Being fearless is almost the philosophy of our day, and in one sense at least it's admirable. It is a good thing to live free of the paralyzing pain of fear. No man can be all he should be if he is frozen by fear. It will keep him from making good decisions for himself and others.

But there is a freedom from fear that is not appropriate—it's having no fear of authority and no fear of consequences. In extreme sports, for example, it means that you ignore the law of gravity at your peril! Ultimately, that kind of lack of respect for rule and responsibility is found in a widespread lack of fear of God. Yet the Bible is clear that a high regard for God is absolutely vital if we are to hope to be able to make good decisions and live well. Proverbs 1:7 (NASB) declares, "The fear of the Lord is the beginning of knowledge; fools despise wisdom and instruction." This kind of fear will guide a man's steps.

Fearing God in the right way is perhaps the most fundamental and foundational thing a man can do to become all he should. It is centered on his role as priest—knowing, loving, and serving God, then leading others into the same relationship. But what does it mean to "fear God" in a healthy way? It is not living with the idea that God has a big stick or hammer and is waiting to smash you over the head for the least little thing you might do wrong. I am not talking about being afraid of being in the presence of God or of coming to God.

As a loving, merciful Father, God calls us to "draw near to the throne of grace, that we may receive mercy and find grace to help in time of need" (Heb. 4:16, ESV). Clearly, the Bible does not teach that the fear of the Lord is like cowering away from an abusive father. On the contrary, the fear of the Lord is having a conscious awareness that God is watching and that you can approach Him for help, particularly when you're facing difficult situations.

> Fearing God in the right way is perhaps the most fundamental and foundational thing a man can do to become all he should.

However, this is where many people get off track and lead countless people astray. There are those who teach people to approach God as though He is just "one of the boys" or as if He is "a man like we are." Some have even taught that when you are in the presence of God, you are free to do weird and preposterous things that are unbiblical. Such behavior shows great disrespect for the dignity of a holy God who does all things decently and in order. There is a difference between having an intimate relationship with someone and being irreverent in front of them.

No, fearing the Lord means living in such a manner that you want to do nothing to displease or disappoint God. Why? Because you respect Him so much and because you are so thankful and grateful for His love, mercy, grace, peace, joy, provision, and protection. The fear of the Lord is cherishing the thought of bowing down to and before God in awe and wonder, in respect for Who He is, the awesome Creator of the universe Who is in total and complete control.

To fear the Lord means to revere, honor, and have a healthy respect for the Lord God because you recognize Him as worthy of the utmost esteem. You are astonished by Him and His love and care for you, and in response your greatest desire is to please Him only. This is more than just a concept, or something to which you give mental assent. It's not merely an intellectual acknowledgment—it is an awareness, an orientation that expresses itself in a willful, daily surrender to God and His will.

Living in healthy fear of the Lord is not simply a divine suggestion. The scriptures clearly say that you and I are commanded to fear God. Deuteronomy 10:12 (NKJV) says, "And now, Israel, what does the Lord your God require of you, but to fear the Lord your God, to walk in all His ways and to love Him, to serve the Lord your God with all your heart and with all your soul."

THE REWARDS OF RESPECT

Fearing God and teaching others to do the same is not a one-way thing. God is gracious and full of compassion, and He has chosen to compensate or reward those who live in the fear of Him. He does not have to give us anything. He does not have to move on our behalf or show us kindness. But because He is a covenant-keeping God who loves with an unconditional love, He will reward all those who live in reverence, awe, honor, and respect of Him and His Word. As the Psalmist wrote, "Blessed is the man who fears the Lord ... " (Ps. 112:1, NKJV). Later, in verse 7, the writer adds, "He will not be afraid."

Men, when you fear the Lord, you need not fear anything else. The fear of God is the fear that conquers every other fear! Notice what blessings and benefits there are to the family when the husband, the father, the man of the house walks in the fear of the Lord. Verse 1 says he is "blessed who fears the Lord."

There is happiness or contentment for the man who fears God. Whatever other men may think of them or say about them, God says they are blessed! Indeed, there are four blessings that come to the man who fears the Lord, which, in turn, are transferred to his family.

> **M**en, when you fear the Lord, you need not fear anything else. The fear of God is the fear that conquers every other fear!

WHEN A MAN FEARS THE LORD:

His Children Will Be Powerful

It is said of the man who shows reverence, respect, honor, and esteem toward God that "his descendants will be mighty on earth" (Ps. 112:2, NKJV). Perhaps he himself will not be so great in the world; maybe he won't make the cover of *TIME* magazine. But his seed, his sons and his daughters after him, shall be mighty. The word "mighty" means that they will not grow up being weak, lacking faith, knowing little if anything about the grace of God. It means that they will not grow up and fall by the wayside or live godless lives. The word literally means *powerful*, with the implication that they will be champions who excel, who are strong and valiant.

A man who fears the Lord will protect and establish future generations. Martin Luther King, Jr., was a man who "feared the Lord" in its proper sense. His son, and now his son's sons and daughters, are becoming "mighty" on the earth. Psalm 112:2 continues, "The generation of the upright will be blessed...." That is, if they walk in the steps of fathers who fear the Lord. Too many men these days are trying to be somebody important only for their own sense of meaning and purpose. They have no time to invest in their children so they can have a healthy fear of God and grow up mighty.

His Family Will Prosper

To the man who will "fear the Lord," the scriptures promise that his family, his household, shall prosper both materially and spiritually. They shall be blessed with outward prosperity; not meaning that they necessarily get everything they want, but according to what they need to be a blessing to others. A man who fears the Lord will protect his family from poverty and need. In the psalms, the writer says, "Wealth and riches will be in the house" (Ps. 112:3, NKJV). It will be in your "house"—that is, in your family heritage. A man who fears the Lord will receive blessings that he will be able to pass on to his children, thus securing their future.

That same verse goes on to say that such a man's righteousness "shall endure forever." His family will be blessed with the true riches of spiritual blessings. It has been said, "Grace is better than gold, because when your gold is gone, grace will live on." Worldly prosperity is a blessing only when it does not cause you to lose your "fear of God." A true, godly man can bless his family with wealth and still persevere in the fruits of the Spirit—"love, joy, peace, long-suffering, kindness, goodness, faithfulness, gentleness, and self-control" (Gal. 5:22–23, NKJV). Such a family is blessed indeed.

His Family Will Be Protected

When a family faces dark and difficult times, the man who fears the Lord will not ignore his troubles or seek to bail out of the situation. Instead, he will bring "light" or comfort to his family in their hour of affliction. God's promises do not exempt a family from affliction just because the father fears the Lord. All families will have their share of the common calamities of life, but the good news is that when these trials come to a family that walks in the fear of the Lord, He will not only *bring* them light, He will *be* their light.

Any time a family faces a crisis—whether it is in relation to health, career, finances, or relationships—life can be hard. However, one of the reasons so many families never recover from a crisis is that their men do not fear the Lord and therefore have no faith in Him to bring them out. Many of those fathers abandon their families when the going gets tough. But the man who fears the Lord teaches his family how to release faith in the tough times and teaches his family to "walk by faith and not by sight" (2 Cor. 5:7, NASB). He teaches them to trust the Lord, Who will watch over them.

His Decisions Will Be Prudent

When men walk in the fear of the Lord, they have godly wisdom for managing all their affairs and concerns. Rather than having to rely on miracles, you will see God increase your goods and bless your family through wise and prudent decisions He helps you make. With God as your teacher and instructor, you will be able to guide and handle your business affairs with discretion, honor, and integrity.

Men who do not fear the Lord will tend to make selfish decisions that hurt rather than help their families. They will not take into consideration all the implications of their decisions. They will refuse to listen to the counsel of their wives, pastors, or trusted advisors and will ultimately make choices that cause hurt, pain, and unnecessary hardships. In contrast, a man who fears the Lord will use wisdom and discernment in managing his affairs, in getting and saving, so that he may have something to give. He shows favor and lends. Psalm 112:5 (NKJV) says that such a man will "will guide his affairs with discretion."

In other words, he has good judgment. A man who fears the Lord does not only guide his business affairs and family decisions with discretion; he will also choose his words with care. He will use discernment in what he shares in the presence of his family. He will not say any and everything in the presence of his children. He will speak life and not death, blessing and not cursing into their lives. These are the kinds of priestly men we need in these days—men who know how to walk in the fear of the Lord. They are the men who will protect their families effectively and consistently in these changing times.

WHEN PRIESTS GO MISSING

In the third chapter of Isaiah, we see what happens when priests do not fulfill their role, when their spiritual leadership is lost. The situation is similar to that of our day and time. Israel was a sick nation, with a morally corrupt society. They were people who had seen great prosperity, and they enjoyed political prominence during the seventh and eighth centuries. Their economic and political power led them to forget about the God of their fathers. They forgot that it was He who had brought them out of bondage and who was the source of all their blessings. They bowed down and worshipped idols, while oppressing the poor and neglecting the elderly, the widows, and the orphans.

Having once walked closely with the Lord, the people of Israel now abused His sanctuary and entertained false prophets. They neglected to teach their children the Word and the ways of God, and they forgot to honor Him in all their ways. They divorced their wives for any reason. They neglected their children, and on many occasions even sacrificed them in the fire to the false Ammonite god called Molech. As a result, the people became very corrupt. Violence, oppression, and immorality swept the nation. Things got so bad that God cried out to the prophet, "I looked and there was no one to help, and I wondered that there was no one to uphold" (Isa. 63:5, NKJV).

The nation suffered. The families suffered. The religious community suffered. The economy and all the land began to fail because God could not find one man who would stand up and take his rightful place as His answer to the problems of society.

Men, today your society, family, community, and church are all suffering and are on the brink of total destruction—unless

God can count on you to become the leader He designed you to be. In Isaiah 3:1–5, God warns He will take away the supply and the support. When men refuse to lead and care for their families and take control of the culture, God says He will take away the food supply, the water, and the staples of the economy.

In addition, God says He will take away the role models, the heroes, the warriors, the judges, the prophets, the elders, the counselors, the skilled craftsmen, the orators, the writers, the men who are thinkers, and the men of rank or ability. Then, in verse 12, God says He will allow boys to become the officials and will allow the women and children to rule over the society. This seems to be more and more the condition of our culture today!

> Men, today your society, family, community, and church are all suffering and are on the brink of total destruction—unless God can count on you to become the leader He designed you to be.

When men refuse to lead, there will be no true leadership in the land. The greatest problem in America today is not that sinners are sinning. The greatest problem is that men are not leading, that our priests have gone missing.

PRIESTS IN THE HOME

While we are to give honor and respect to those in authority over us, the moral and spiritual leadership needed in our world today cannot come from those who do not know God, no matter how famous or influential they may be. They cannot truly lead until they know how to serve God. The leadership that will turn the hearts of fathers to their children and the hearts of children to their fathers and cause the land to be spared the wrath of God begins in the home. It will come from men who step up and into their role as priest—those who pray and make intercession on behalf of others.

> When men refuse to lead, there will be no true leadership in the land. The greatest problem in America today is not that sinners are sinning. The greatest problem is that men are not leading, that our priests have gone missing.

Many men these days want to be recognized as the king of their castle, but they do not deserve to lead before they know how to serve. You can't become a king without first serving as a priest. It is true that every member of the body of Christ is called to be a priest unto God, to offer praise and thanksgiving, to study and walk in His ways, and to demonstrate His love to others. However, men hold a unique role of priest in the family. This is not to say that a wife, a mother, or children cannot and should not come to God on their own. But as the children or the wife come to God, they can come under the protection of the father. As a man, you are to be the priest in the home, representing your family before God.

As the priest in your home, you are called to teach and model for your family how to:

- Know God.
- Love God.
- Serve God.

This is what King David charged his son, Solomon, with as he prepared to pass on his kingdom. 1 Kings 2:3 (ESV) records David saying, "And keep the charge of the LORD your God, walking in his ways and keeping his statutes, his commandments, his rules, and his testimonies, as it is written in the Law of Moses, that you may prosper in all that you do and wherever you turn." In other words, David was saying, "Son, your relationship with God, loving and honoring His Word, following and trusting Him—that is the main thing in life that matters."

As priest, you must teach and demonstrate to your family that it is good and right to:

- Love God...because He is God!

- Trust God...because He is faithful to His Word!

- Obey God...because He loves your family members and wants them to prosper!

The greatest single role a priest has is to make intercession for others. Just as Jesus is our High Priest, seated at the right hand of the Father, ever making intercession for us, so, too, a man is the priest who stands in the presence of Christ on behalf of his family.

I believe that if every father would earnestly intercede for his children, we could turn our world around in almost no time. When a husband understands his responsibility and the power of his intercession, he will lay on his face before God on behalf of his family and their needs. A godly man teaches his family to pray by example, by praying for them and with them. Five-star General Douglas MacArthur, the famous American hero of World War II, put it this way:

> By profession I am a soldier and take pride in that fact. But I am prouder—infinitely prouder—to be a father. A soldier destroys in order to build; the father only builds, never destroys. The one has the potentiality of death; the other embodies creation and life. And while the hordes of death are mighty, the battalions of life are mightier still. It is my hope

that my son, when I am gone, will remember me
not from the battle but in the home repeating with
him our simple daily prayer, Our Father Who Art
in Heaven.[1]

An important key here is that a man who fears the Lord,
who is serving his family as priest, will be willing to become
the answer to his own prayers on their behalf. He will sacrifice
himself as the answer to their needs. This is the kind of true
faith into which men are called to lead their families as priests.
I am not talking about false faith that simply goes through the
motions of prayer without power.

I mean real faith that fights for the family and takes back
what has been stolen. Faith that is based on a word from God
and on the assurance that He will do it because He said it and
because He is God. It is a faith in the living Lord Jesus Christ,
who came that you and your family might have life and have
it more abundantly.

CALL TO ACTION: IDENTIFYING
WITH THE PRIEST

A man's mind is typically set on three things; his job, his
money, and his pleasure. These are the things he usually rever-
ences. This causes a major problem because relationships with
his wife, family, church, and community are neglected.

When a man taps into the power of being a priest, his focus
changes. As he gives reverence to God, his world is expanded
and God orchestrates the affairs of his life.

Men, our thought life has to be more God-focused. We
need His help, even though pride tells us to continue to believe
the lie, "I got this!"

Make this commitment to trusting God a part of your daily
prayer life. Offer this simple prayer, which can and should be
recited throughout your day: "Lord, I reverence you. I need
you to help me to be the total man I need to be. Help me

reprioritize the affairs of my life so that you will be glorified and I will find fulfillment. Amen!"

As priest, you change "what" you reverence to "who" you reverence. By so doing you position yourself to lead your household in godly fear.

Chapter Fourteen:

THE PROPHET: SPEAKING IDENTITY, CASTING VISION

I F A MAN'S most important role in his home and community is as priest, then the second is his call to be a prophet. What's the difference? A priest is one who goes before God on behalf of someone else. A prophet, on the other hand, is one who comes to someone on behalf of God.

As a husband, father, friend, and peer, you need not only bring others to God in prayer; you have a responsibility to bring His word to them. Prophets speak identity and cast vision. They declare what should be, what can be, and what will be. They bring words of encouragement and instruction, and sometimes words of admonishment. Ever since Adam, every man has had within him the power to be a vision-caster for himself and his family. Remember from the Genesis account that the responsibility for casting the vision was not given to Eve; she was not yet brought forth.

> As a husband, father, friend, and peer, you need not only bring others to God in prayer; you have a responsibility to bring His word to them.

It is the responsibility of the man, the husband, the father, to communicate (cast) the vision to his wife, the rest of the family, and the community. What happens when men refuse this responsibility? Proverbs 29:18 (KJV) says, "Where there is no vision, the people perish...." In other words, when a man has no vision for his family and their future, he will lower his expectations and standards and he will allow them to do whatever they want…without values or direction.

Men are supposed to be guardians of the vision, as Adam was to hold to God's plan for the Garden. It was to be a place where the man and woman could experience God's total "Shalom"—well-being, health, wealth, peace, harmony, and love. That is still our role today. We must guard the vision of living in a society that values all the good things that God said we could and should enjoy. The passage in 1 Timothy 6:17 (NKJV) says it is God "who gives us richly all things to enjoy." Men with this prophetic quality are sorely missed in our world today. Just look around at how many young people are growing up with no clear sense of who they are and where they are going.

> It is not enough simply to go to church; we need to be in touch with God constantly, hearing His voice, listening to His commands, and following His directions. If we don't, we will make the mistake that Adam made—we will lose

A PROPHET'S PLACE

Though the need for prophets is great, it is no small thing to be given the responsibility of going to someone else on God's behalf. The role of prophet can be fulfilled properly only if men understand where and how they need to be rooted to flourish in this responsibility. God set the man in the Garden of Eden—a particular place for a particular purpose. God set the man in the environment in which he was supposed to remain to fulfill his reason for being.

The place was the Garden of Eden. The word for "garden," as I have noted previously, means "an enclosure" or "something fenced in"—which makes me think back to the Maasai's *kraals.* Eden was no ordinary garden. It represented the glory of heaven; it was God's incubator for His new children, His new offspring created in His image and after His likeness.

God placed the man there so that he could continually be in His presence. He could walk and talk with the Lord in the cool of the day (Gen. 3:8). Adam could hear the voice of God and commune with Him, fellowship with Him, and be at one with Him always. From that place, in the presence of God, he would be able to be a visionary and a leader, representing the Father's heart and will.

God never intended for Adam to move from or leave the Garden. He intended Eden to expand and cover all of the earth. God wanted Adam to take the presence of the Garden and spread it throughout the world. This is the meaning of the command for Adam to "have dominion over the earth" (Gen. 1:26, 28). Even though this plan suffered a setback, it has not changed. As Adam's descendants, we are to advance the kingdom of God throughout the entire earth today. Isaiah 11:9 (NKJV) says, "For the earth shall be full of the knowledge of the Lord, as the waters cover the sea."

God gave the man this vision of what the world should look like and what the world should be like under his leadership and authority. God transferred that authority to Adam. In Genesis 2:15, 19-20 (NKJV) we read, "Then the LORD God took the man and put him in the Garden of Eden to tend and keep it.... Out of the ground the LORD God formed every beast of the field and every bird of the air, and brought them to Adam to see what he would call them. And whatever Adam called each living creature, that was its name. So Adam gave names to all cattle, to the birds of the air, and to every beast of the field."

As a result, Adam, who had been given the vision and the authority, was placed in the position of leader. He was to carry out the plan of God to extend and enclose the entire earth with His garden of delight and pleasure. It is clear, however, that Adam was not going to carry out this plan alone with God. He was given a helper created by the work of God. God created woman out of man and gave her to the man as his helper in fulfilling the vision of God for mankind.

Men, we must understand our position. It is to be in the presence of God at all times. It is not enough simply to go to church; we need to be in touch with God constantly, hearing His voice, listening to His commands, and following His directions. If we don't, we will make the mistake that Adam made—we will lose sight of the vision, get out of position, and forfeit our authority to carry out God's plan. Remember, the first thing God gave the man He created was not a woman, not a job; it was not even a command. The first thing God gave was His Presence—His breath of life and His garden of delight and pleasure. Our position as men is to be the visionary leaders who stay in the presence of God so we can extend His garden, His will, and His kingdom throughout the entire earth.

A PROPHET'S PURPOSE

As prophet, a man is to "forth tell" the word of God to his family. The Bible teaches that he is to exhort and encourage them to live lives of holiness and to walk worthy of their calling. He is to let them know what God expects of them and what he has learned in prayer as he has sought God's will. It is in prayer, in God's presence, that he discovers God's vision for his family and then is able to encourage and direct them toward God's purposes. It was Adam who was to tell Eve, "Thus said the Lord." He was to be the prophet in the Garden, to bring God's Word into reality and manifestation. He was to listen to God, not to his wife, when it came time to make the decision to eat of the tree of the knowledge of good and evil.

Unfortunately, Adam decided to abdicate his position of prophet and abandon his place of spiritual leadership. Far too many men are following in Adam's careless footsteps these days. They may not have abandoned their families physically—though too many have—but they have deserted them spiritually and mentally.

Today, men have become extremely self-centered, sometimes without even knowing it. They are too focused on prophesying over their own lives instead of praying and prophesying over the lives of others they are responsible for. We have adopted an "I have to get mine first" attitude, which has been reinforced by "get rich quick" TV shows and prosperity preaching. Thus, men pray primarily for their own success and believe every divine message they receive is for them. I have news for men who are true believers: every divine message you receive from God is not necessarily for you! Remember, prophets foretell God's word to others—are you hijacking someone else's prophecy?

FATHERS ARE NATURAL PROPHETS

Too many men are leaving the teaching of the Word of God, the praying to God, the promoting of godly morals and values, and the worship of God to their wives. But men are to be the prophets in the home, leading their families in worship, praise, and thanksgiving to God. They are to lead their families in the study of God's Word, in witnessing to the lost, and in sharing in missions. They are the ones who should be leading and showing the way.

Unless men become more than Sunday-morning church visitors, our children will become a generation that does not know the Lord. The Bible warns that this generation, which knows more about YouTube, blogging, texting, and Instagram than about the things of God, is in danger of becoming rebellious and violently lost.

According to Proverbs 30:11–14 (NKJV), "There is a generation that curses its father, and does not bless its mother. There is a generation that is pure in its own eyes, yet is not washed from its filthiness. There is a generation—oh, how lofty are their eyes! And their eyelids are lifted up. There is a generation whose teeth are like swords, and whose fangs are like knives, to devour the poor from off the earth, and the needy from among men."

> Unless men become more than Sunday-morning church visitors, our children will become a generation that does not know the Lord.

These young people need prophetic fathers who will impart spiritual truth and godly wisdom into their lives. Now is not the time to shy away from this generation; rather, this is the time to become like the prophets of old, who were consumed with their message and passionate about being faithful to deliver what God was saying.

A PROPHET'S NAME

In the natural order, men are called to be providers, but it goes far beyond just ensuring the basic necessities of life. Above all, men are to provide stability, security, and a sense of identity for the family. Traditionally, when the man and woman stood at the marriage altar, they became "Mr. and Mrs." She took his name.

Just as Adam named the woman "Eve," when a man and woman marry today, usually he (the husband) literally names her (the wife). She leaves the name of her birth and takes the name of his birth. What an awesome responsibility the man now has: the children will have his name. He will be the source of the family's identity. He will bring them up to the level of his name—or he can take them down to the level of his name.

Men, you cannot escape this truth. Whether you are in the home or not, you are responsible for the identity of your offspring, and you provide them with their sense of self-esteem. It may be good or it may be bad, but your name is the source of identity for your family. The identity we provide is the character we are building into their lives by our interactions in their lives. We must take advantage of everything that happens in their lives. We can use all those situations to create life lessons, teachable moments that will affect the way they live in the future.

Another way in which we provide and shape our children's identity is by reminding them that they are loved, valued, and accepted for who they are, not for what they might look like or their achievements.

I recall a story that I was told that is a perfect example of this principle. As the story goes, a young boy named Jimmy was playing for a soccer championship title. Though the kids were only five and six years old, they took it very seriously— as did some of the parents. Determined to win the match, at halftime the other team's coach refused to switch out all of his first-choice players who had started the game so that rest of his squad had a chance to play, as the rules of the league directed.

That left Jimmy as goalkeeper for the team playing by the rules, soon overrun by the superior skills of their opponents. Though he was good for his age, Jimmy was simply no match for those on the other team because of the advantage they were enjoying.

The opposing side began to score. One goal came after another; poor Jimmy simply could not stop the barrage of shots coming at him. He gave it his all, recklessly throwing his body in front of incoming balls, trying valiantly, but the other team kept finding the back of the net.

Jimmy's parents were watching from the sidelines. Still wearing his suit and tie, the boy's father looked as though he had rushed over to the game straight from the office. He yelled encouragement to his son, urging him to try harder, and shouting advice. After the fourth and fifth goals, Jimmy slumped. He could see it was no use; he couldn't stop the other team on his own. He didn't quit, but he became quietly desperate. Futility and frustration were written all over his face.

Jimmy's father changed, too. He became anxious for his son, yelling that it was okay, encouraging him to hang in there. But the onslaught continued. After retrieving the ball from the net for the eighth time, Jimmy handed it to the referee and then broke down and cried. He stood there as huge tears rolled down both cheeks. Then he went to his knees—and that is when his father stepped up.

Jimmy's mother tried to stop her husband. Perhaps she thought that he was angry with their son, and concerned that he would yell at the boy and embarrass him even more. But the man pulled free and dashed onto the field, even though the game was still in progress.

He didn't care about the rules, nor about how he looked. Suit, tie, dress shoes, and all, he charged onto the field, ran over to the goal area where his son was kneeling, and scooped the boy up in his arms so everybody would know that Jimmy was his. He hugged and kissed his son—and cried with him.

He carried the boy off the field, and as they got close to the sidelines, he said to his son, "Jimmy, I'm so proud of you. You were great out there. I want everybody to know that you are my son."

The boy sobbed. "Daddy," he said, "I couldn't stop them. I tried, Daddy, I tried and tried, but they kept scoring on me."

The man hugged his son. "Jimmy, it doesn't matter how many times they score on you," he told him. "You're my son, and I'm proud of you. Now, I want you to go back out there and finish the game. I know you want to quit, but you can't. And son, you're going to get scored on again, but it doesn't matter. You are still my son!"

It was a different little Jimmy who ran back onto the field. His confidence had been restored, and his self-image was intact because he knew that his identity was not determined by his performance. And, yes, the other team scored twice more, but, it was okay—Jimmy had been reminded who and whose he was, and that changed everything.

Such is the prophetic role of a man, a father, speaking life and hope to those in his world. God also gave Adam the vision and the command to provide direction and destiny for those who would come after him; remember, he was the recipient of all the information, revelation, and communication from his heavenly Father. God's purpose was to have an orderly transfer of His commands from Adam to all those who were of his family. A man who has no God-given vision for life will destroy his family quicker than anything from the outside. The vision for a harmonious society, the vision of dominion, replenishment, and continual fellowship with God, was given to men in the person of Adam. It is the responsibility of fathers to keep this vision alive and transfer it into the lives of their children and their children's children.

A PROPHET'S DIRECTION

Too many children and teens today are struggling with what to do with their lives because they have not been given any sense of direction. In the absence of their fathers' instruction and words from other godly men, they are turning to gangs and violence, drugs, and premarital sex for a sense of purpose, meaning, and belonging.

> The vision for a harmonious society, the vision of dominion, replenishment, and continual fellowship with God, was given to men in the person of Adam. It is the responsibility of fathers to keep this vision alive and transfer it into the lives of their children and their children's children.

Men who stand as prophets in their homes and communities know how to help their families, as well as other young men and women who may be without a father or father figure, discover their gifts and abilities. They know how to breathe vision into their children's lives. As they help them discover their gifts, they then provide direction in the development of those gifts. They will actively get children in their sphere of influence involved in activities to teach them life skills that will serve them in their adult lives. Through their direction and encouragement, they give their children the courage and passion to be more than they ever imagined they could be. They actively encourage every effort their children make to increase their self-confidence.

My father gave me and my brothers, Tony, William, and Rodney, the opportunity to get both religious and academic training by insisting that our mother keep us in parochial schools. Each of us graduated from Purcell High School in Cincinnati. Tony and I went on to graduate from Xavier University of Cincinnati, while William and Rodney graduated from the University of Cincinnati. We were the first in our family line to graduate from college.

George and my mother worked together to see to it that their sons grew up with an academic as well as a moral foundation. George provided a pathway for us to be able to reach our destiny. It was his unspoken prophecy over our lives. He had the "spirit of fatherhood," even though there were times when his physical presence was missing. He was our foundation, and because of our parents' commitment to each of their sons, we are now raising our families with a solid foundation of unconditional love and commitment.

The responsibility to help children become all they can is ultimately not something that we can just pass off to others. Nor is it just teaching about things and activities. Children have many potential male teachers who can direct them into the careers they should pursue in life. But such instructors, valuable as they are, cannot give our children what a prophet-father can—a sense of their true destiny in Christ.

The Apostle Paul said in 1 Corinthians 4:15 (NKJV), "For though you might have ten thousand instructors in Christ, yet you do not have many fathers." Good fathers will link their families to the heavenly Father, who will reveal His ultimate plans for their lives. They will teach their families how to hear the voice of the Lord, and encourage them to follow it, no matter how challenging that word might be.

> Children have many potential male teachers who can direct them into the careers they should pursue in life. But such instructors, valuable as they are, cannot give our children what a prophet-father can—a sense of their true destiny in Christ.

Just as Jesus said to His followers, *"follow me,"* and as Paul urged his sons and daughters in the faith to *"follow me and imitate me,"* so, too, can fathers say to their children, "Follow me and imitate me." This sense of direction and destiny is something a teacher cannot give.

The radiant reflection of children is their father; he represents all they can be and more. In the father they see their hopes fulfilled, their destiny complete, and their dreams realized. Fathers are the glory of their children because they are the foundation for all that they will do in life.

As Paul wrote in Philippians 4:9 (NKJV), fathers should exhort their children, "The things which you learned and received and heard and saw in me, these do...." Whatever the father does, even in the home, says to the children, "You follow me, and I will show you the way. I am the pathfinder, pioneer, and discoverer, and I am preparing a way for you that is worthy to follow."

A PROPHET'S PRIORITY

Just as children may have many instructors but only one father, they can also have a lot of friends. Too many men today are focused more on being their children's friend than being their father. I am not saying there is no time or place for friendship between fathers and their children. But we have lost sight of what is most important, about what is primary. We have raised a generation of children who are addicted to entertainment, and in doing so, many fathers make the mistake of trying to be their children's best friend and entertainer. This is not your role! Your God-given position is to be a priest and a prophet in the lives of your children, directing and guiding them into the Word of God and into a life that is honoring to Him.

In times of old, the prophet was God's representative to His people. It's still the same: men, you represent God to those you have influence over and specifically as a father, you represent God to your children. You will shape their image of God by the example you are providing for them. This means that you are to reveal by your very character the way God desires to relate to the world and, in particular, to your children. This means standing true to God and what He has said, even when it is not easy, convenient, or necessarily preferable. But as prophets, we are called to be men of faith. Perhaps the most important thing you can pass on to your children is faith. Why? Because without faith it is impossible to please God (Heb. 11:6), and it is by faith that they will overcome the world (1 John 5:4).

Satan targets your home to get to your faith. When he attacked Job, it was for the express purpose of destroying his faith in God. But Job maintained his faith and said, "Though He slay me, yet will I trust Him" (Job 13:15, NKJV). Men, when you are under attack, that is not the time to give up and give in; that is the time to reveal to your children the power of the prophetic anointing that God has given you as a man of God. It is the time to say to your children, "Things are tough right now, but I trust God, and I am fully persuaded that God will grant us favor, and we will come out of this as winners."

My dad always encouraged us to look to the future, even though times were tough. When we had to eat pork-n-beans and cube steaks for weeks and weeks at a time, he would constantly remind us that things would get better, and one day we would be able to eat whatever we wanted because of our education and hard work. Men, when you are consistent in your words of encouragement and affirmation, you are transferring your faith to your children and teaching them that "He [God] will not leave you nor forsake you..." (Deut. 31:8, NKJV) and that they can always depend on the faithfulness of God.

When your wife and children see a demonstration of your faith in the hard seasons, it prepares them to go through the storms, the fires, and the valley of the shadow of death with confidence in God, confidence in themselves, and confidence in you as their priest and prophet.

CALL TO ACTION: OBTAINING THE VOICE AND VISION OF THE PROPHET

Attending church with your family is a great start. The all-too-common mistake that many men make, however, is leaving the spiritual nurturing of their family to the pastor, the Sunday school teacher, and their wives.

Whether you are listening to a sermon, attending a Bible study, or reading the Bible for yourself, consider these points:

1. Receive the Word for a personal application. As you become "a doer of the Word," it becomes more obvious to your family, and this gives credence to your spiritual voice and vision.

2. Listen to the Word with an eye to your family's needs. Maybe you've heard the sermon before or know the scripture passage quite well. That doesn't mean your family does. Don't tune out, but tune in to obtain information that you can use as object lessons with your family.

3. Have discussions with your family about the sermon or other things you have learned through personal or corporate Bible study. Asking how they enjoyed the service is just the kick-off into a deeper conversation. When they see that you take it seriously enough to discuss it, the Word of God becomes more credible in their eyes.

4. Project it forward. So often the spiritual conversations we have with our families revolve around "What did you learn? What did you get out of it?" Change the conversation to ask questions like, "How will you apply this? How does this impact the goals you have set for your life? Do you feel this is relevant to your future?"

As you have these conversations, questions will arise that will cause you to study the Bible and pray more. Ask God for guidance, and increase your meditation time on the Word as you study. This will help you obtain your prophetic voice and vision. Then, as you continue your conversations, you can share your knowledge, encouragement, and admonishment. The word of God that you live out and speak into others is transformational in both your life and theirs. As you witness spiritual growth in yourself and your family, you will realize that you have tapped into something very special and powerful.

Chapter Fifteen

THE PATTERN: LIVING AS AN EXAMPLE

WHEN IT COMES to leadership, there are those who merely *tell* others what to do and how to do it, and there are those who *show* others what to do and how to do it. Which do you think is more successful? Showing, of course. You have no doubt heard the phrase, "It's better to walk the walk than talk the talk." But even better is walking *and* talking, showing *and* telling. And that is the kind of leadership men have been called to exercise in their homes, churches, and communities. Not just, "Do as I say" but "Do as I do."

Men have found themselves repeating patterns of behavior like rituals and traditions since the days of Abraham. This following patterns, mimicking others, can be good or bad—depending on who or what you set as your example. How does one determine what a good example is? That's an easy answer: good examples always honor God in spirit and in truth. This is important to remember because repeating activities simply for the sake of tradition is meaningless to God.

There are many biblical examples for men to pattern themselves after. However, the one true example is Jesus Christ. As I noted earlier, it was God's plan all along to have His Son's life become an example to all men of the kind of relationship we should have with the Father.

Men are responsible for effectively conveying the intricacies of the Father's will to the world. We have been entrusted with the word of God, and it is our place to make sure that we serve as examples that our families can pattern themselves after. Fathers, through their words and actions, are to teach their children the will and the ways of God.

Furthermore, while it is important for men to understand that what they *tell* others is significant, even more impactful is how they *show* them. Who do you pattern yourself after? Does someone who knows and honors God come to mind? The most important thing you can teach others is not *what* you know about God but *that* you know God personally and, in turn, are known by Him. With that in mind, would you feel comfortable if your children or someone you were mentoring wanted to pattern their life after yours?

> The most important thing you can teach others is not what you know about God but that you know God personally and, in turn, are known by Him.

Consider Stephen, one of the first martyrs of the early church. Others had what might be considered more important tasks, needing to devote themselves to prayer and preaching. Stephen and several others were appointed to handle some of the practical needs of the new believers, to free up the elders to focus on the word of God. But Stephen lived in such a way that God blessed him with the highest compliment given to any man other than Enoch, who just walked with God into glory. Stephen was a man of such vision, virtue, and values that when he died, serving the Lord with boldness, Jesus didn't sit down and receive him into glory—Jesus stood up and gave Stephen a standing ovation (Acts 7:54-60). What was one of the qualities that set Stephen apart? When he was selected for his distribution duties, he was chosen as a man "full of the Holy Spirit and wisdom" (Acts 6:3, NKJV).

Above all, fulfilling a spiritual role requires men to be spiritual. You cannot deliver to others what you have not received. Speaking to God and hearing from God demands a certain spirituality that is not attained overnight. The good news is that we are not alone in what we have been given to do. The Holy Spirit has been given to empower and guide all of us. When Jesus ascended to His Father, He promised that He would send the Comforter (John 14:26), Who would be with us at all times and Who would guide us into all truth.

The Comforter is the communicator on behalf of God. By His presence, He can help you fulfill your role as priest and prophet in your family and as God's man in the world at large. The Holy Spirit is our *"helper,"* the *"other comforter"* sent by the Father to continue the work of Jesus, who completed His mission on earth and is now seated at the right hand of the Father, ever making intercession for you and me. The Holy Spirit has now come into the world and permanently dwells in every born-again believer. He has come to be to us everything that Jesus was to the apostles and His early disciples during His earthly ministry. Just as Jesus told His disciples, "Without Me you can do nothing" (John 15:5, NKJV), the same holds true in our relationship with the Holy Spirit.

Without the Holy Spirit actively leading and guiding us, we can do nothing worthwhile for the kingdom of God, and we cannot fulfill our spiritual role. It is worth noting that when Jesus faced one of His biggest tests, He did so "full of the Holy Spirit":

> Jesus, full of the Holy Spirit, returned from the Jordan and was led around by the Spirit in the wilderness for forty days, being tempted by the devil. And He ate nothing during those days, and when they had ended, He became hungry. And the devil said to Him, "If You are the Son of God, tell this stone to become bread." And Jesus answered him, "It is written, 'Man shall not live on bread alone.'" And he led Him up and showed Him all the kingdoms of the world in a moment of time. And the devil said to Him, "I will give You all this domain and its glory; for it has been

handed over to me, and I give it to whomever I wish. Therefore, if You worship before me, it shall all be Yours." Jesus answered and said to him, "It is written, 'You shall worship the Lord your God and serve Him only.'" And he led Him to Jerusalem and had Him stand on the pinnacle of the temple and said to Him, "If You are the Son of God, throw Yourself down from here; for it is written, 'He will command His angels concerning You to guard You, and, on their hands they will bear You up, so that you will not strike Your foot against a stone.'" And Jesus answered and said to him, "It is said, 'You shall not put the Lord your God to the test.'" When the devil had finished every temptation, he left Him until an opportune time. And Jesus returned to Galilee in the power of the Spirit; and news about Him spread through all the surrounding district (Luke 4:1–14, NASB).

> Without the Holy Spirit actively leading and guiding us, we can do nothing worthwhile for the kingdom of God, and we cannot fulfill our spiritual role.

I don't know about you, but I have a hunger, a thirst, a burning desire to be continuously filled with the Spirit of God. I want to be like my namesake, the Apostle Philip, who, after his conversion, desired to share the word of God with his family, friends, and strangers–essentially becoming a Spirit-led evangelist. I want to be filled with the Spirit of Christ Jesus to the point that I desire only what our heavenly Father desires. I am burdened about the lack of desperation, hunger, and thirst for the things of God in the lives of so many men today. God's plan is for us to be living examples for those we encounter daily. God has called men to be leaders in this world, to be examples of what it means to be saints and bold soldiers of the Lord Jesus Christ.

Our families need Spirit-filled husbands and fathers. The world has enough men filled with the spirit of greed, envy, and sexual perversion, to name just a few unholy habits. The world is in need of real spiritual men to arise in entertainment, sports, the arts, the sciences, education, law, and government. Where are the spiritual men who can heal the crises in the home and the conflicts in our world?

What the world and the church need today are more men whose lives are filled with the Spirit of Jesus Christ, who provides the limitless resources that are given to all believers, allowing them to rise above life's circumstances. Jesus is our primary example of what it means to be a Spirit-filled man. Luke 4:1 says, "Then Jesus, being filled with the Holy Spirit, returned from the Jordan and was led by the Spirit into the wilderness."

To be filled with the Spirit, or to be Spirit-filled, first means that you are saved, that the Holy Spirit has come into your life and taken up permanent residence. It also means you are totally surrendered to His gentle yet firm leading. It means that you allow the Holy Spirit to have complete control over your heart and mind. Every man who is saved has been filled with the Spirit and will not get any more of the Spirit than he already has. So the issue is, how much of your life does the Holy Spirit control?

A man who is filled with the Spirit allows Him within to invade every crack and crevice of his being—every endeavor and every relationship. Your life will exemplify the free and unhindered exercise of all the Holy Spirit's attributes—His knowledge, power, holiness, peace, and joy. If you are a Spirit-filled man, He will reign supreme over your entire life, but not without your permission.

Look at these Spirit-filled men in the Bible and the characteristics they displayed. We need to see these same traits in the lives of God's men today.

LIVING WITH BOLDNESS

"Then Peter, filled with the Holy Spirit...began to speak the word of God with boldness."

—Acts 4:8, 31 (NASB)

LIVING WITH HEAVENLY VISION

"But being full of the Holy Spirit, he [Stephen] gazed intently into heaven and saw the glory of God, and Jesus standing at the right hand of God."

—Acts 7:55 (NASB)

LIVING WITH FAITH

"He [Barnabas] was a good man, and full of the Holy Spirit and of faith."

—Acts 11:24 (NASB)

LIVING WITH AUTHORITY

"Paul, filled with the Holy Spirit, fixed his gaze upon him [Elymas], and said... 'And now, behold, the hand of the Lord is upon you, and you will be blind and not see the sun for a time.' And immediately a mist and a darkness fell upon him, and he went about seeking those who would lead him by the hand."

—Acts 13:9, 11 (NASB)

LIVING WITH JOY

"And the disciples were continually filled with joy and with the Holy Spirit."

—Acts 13:52 (NASB)

Jesus is God, and He does not need anyone or anything. He is Lord of all. So why would Jesus, God in the flesh, come under the control of the Holy Spirit? After all, Jesus could handle the devil, temptations, and life because He was God. The answer is that Jesus was God, but He was also a man. Entering into our world, He put aside every heavenly advantage, and He walked among us in that weak flesh. He knew that to fulfill the Father's will, He must be empowered by the Spirit of His Father. Also, He did it as an example for you and for me.

Jesus knows that, as men, we think there is nothing we cannot handle on our own. The truth is, we must totally and completely surrender our lives to God. Jesus shows us that this is a mandatory step in becoming a "Spirit-filled man." The Bible says He was led by the Spirit (Matt. 4:1). Being led by someone means being surrendered to their leadership, direction, control, and will. That will is in control of where you go, what you do, when you do what you do, and how you do it.

VICTORY THROUGH TOTAL SURRENDER

Men, we cannot continue the lifestyle of talking the same old talk and walking the same old walk. You can keep on trying to figure everything out and make everything work on your own, but you know that you don't have it all together. You know that at any moment, you can lose it and your life will fall apart. As long as you are full of self-believing that you can handle life on your terms, the Holy Spirit will continue to let you live on the roller coaster of uncertainty.

After being born again, the first step to becoming a Spirit-filled man is to recognize that you can't handle life by yourself. The Spirit-filled man is a surrendered man who says, "I cannot make it on my own. I cannot be the kind of man God wants me to be unless I get help." And Jesus said the Helper, the Holy Spirit, is here.

To be a Spirit-filled man is to become totally dependent on

the Holy Spirit. If you have studied the New Testament, it is clear that Jesus had nothing. He owned absolutely nothing. He had no food to depend on for physical strength. He had no friends to depend on for emotional or moral support. He had no transportation except for his two feet. He had no map for the journey and no compass to guide Him.

If you are going to become a Spirit-filled man, you must not only surrender to the Holy Spirit, but you must also become totally dependent on Him. You must depend on Him to help you overcome the temptation to sin, to feed you when you are hungry, and to put you in your proper place in life. You must depend on Him to guide you into truth and to keep you from falling. When you depend on the Holy Spirit to help you become the man of God that He created you to be, you will not be disappointed.

Stop trying futilely to live the Christian life, and be a good husband on your own. Start depending on the Holy Spirit to lead you into what God wants for you and for your family. Stop struggling with the Spirit of God; surrender to and depend on Him to cause you to obey God, live victoriously, and reflect the person of Jesus Christ. Have you ever found yourself bargaining and pleading with God for a spiritual change in your life? Or have you ever felt the need to work harder in the church to please God so that He would give in to your requests?

Today you can live with the full and overflowing presence of the Holy Spirit. Are you willing to become totally dependent and surrendered to God so the Holy Spirit can maximize His work in your life? If you are, God will manifest His Spirit in you as never before. Living this way before others *shows* them the way, rather than merely *telling* them.

> Stop trying futilely to live the Christian life, and be a good husband on your own. Start depending on the Holy Spirit to lead you into what God wants for you and for your family.

Pleasing His heavenly Father was the major motivation in Jesus's life on earth:

> Then Jesus came from Galilee to the Jordan to John to be baptized by him. But John protested strenuously, having in mind to prevent Him, saying, "It is I who have need to be baptized by You, and do You come to me?" But Jesus replied to him, "Permit it just now; for this is the fitting way for [both of] us to fulfill all righteousness [that is, to perform completely whatever is right]." Then he permitted Him. And when Jesus was baptized, He went up at once out of the water; and behold, the heavens were opened, and he [John] saw the Spirit of God descending like a dove and alighting on Him. And behold, a voice from heaven said, "This is My Son, My Beloved, in Whom I delight!" (Matt. 3:13–17, AMP).

Jesus was so motivated and inspired by His Father that He said on one occasion that He would not operate independent of the Father and that He would speak only those things the Father declared (John 5:19, 12:49). One of the greatest ways you can change the world is by living in such a way before others that they seek to emulate you. Many earthly sons and daughters have gone on to live productive and meaningful lives simply because they have always held a picture of their father's approval in their minds.

> "I just owe almost everything to my father, [and] it's passionately interesting for me that the things that I

learned in a small town, in a very modest home, are just the things that I believe have won the election."[1]
—MARGARET THATCHER
FORMER BRITISH PRIME MINISTER

"It's only when you grow up, and step back from him, or leave him for your own career and your own home—it's only then that you measure his greatness and fully appreciate it. Pride reinforces love."[2]
—MARGARET TRUMAN
DAUGHTER OF FORMER
PRESIDENT HARRY S. TRUMAN

"My father taught me that the only way you can make good at anything is to practice, and then practice some more."[3]
—PETE ROSE
FORMER BASEBALL PLAYER

"I will ever be grateful for the wise counsel of a strong and inspired father when he taught, 'If you always say no to the first temptation, you will not have to worry if you will be able to say no to the second one.'"[4]
—HAROLD HILLMAN
PHILOSOPHER

"My father gave me the greatest gift anyone could give another person: he believed in me."[5]
—JIM VALVANO
FORMER COLLEGE BASKETBALL COACH

Just as a man can have a negative impact on his family and others connected to him through the wounds caused by angry words and negative actions, so also can he positively impact them through encouraging words and positive actions—the model of a life lived all-out for God, a life they can pattern theirs after.

CALL TO ACTION: CHANGING THE PATTERN

Men tend to be distant and loners. We *look down* on other men from a distance. We *admire* other men from a distance. We *envy* other men from a distance. That does absolutely nothing for anyone.

Men who have found the kind of success in life that you desire have obviously tapped into something that you haven't. This is nothing to be ashamed of; it's just a fact of life. You can tap into this same power by viewing them not as intense competitors but as an integral component to reaching your goals.

To change this pattern, here are some things you should do:

1. Compliment and celebrate the successes of other men. This helps to squelch that competitive spirit in both of you. It then opens doors for meaningful conversations. Ask, "How did you...?" "Where did you...?" "What can I do to...?"

2. If you are on the receiving end of a compliment, don't just say thank you and gloat. Realize that the man who complimented you has done something difficult for most men. Go out of your way to show yourself friendly, humble, and approachable. If you sense that the man who complimented you is searching for answers in his life, offer your business card, exchange information, and if you sense a connection, consider offering to meet with him for lunch.

3. Identify a man at least ten years younger than you to mentor. Meet regularly to discuss life,

your faith, and issues that relate to manhood. Because you are older, you have life experiences to share with a younger man that can bless him.

4. As you look for a mentor of your own, understand that others' successes did not come without a price. One was probably their efficient use of time. So don't be discouraged if they can't meet as often as you would like. Discussions over lunch or a cup of coffee are the best. But be open to phone calls, e-mails, and text messages.

5. Understand the connection factor. You may meet with a potential mentor, and there may not be a kindred connection. Glean what you can from this person in the handful of encounters you may have, but don't force the issue. Thank him for his contribution and look for someone else to mentor you.

6. Understand the availability factor. You know that guy who appears to have the perfect family and drives the Maserati? Everybody wants him for a mentor! So don't be put off if he tells you he just doesn't have the time.

7. Understand the multitude factor. In the multitude of counselors, your purposes will be established (Prov. 15:22, KJV). It doesn't have to be just one person who mentors you.

Conclusion

THE PRINCIPLES: THIRTEEN STEPS FOR RELEASING YOUR UNTAPPED POWER

I HOPE THAT BY now you are itching to go. I hope you have caught some of the sense of passion and purpose I believe God wants to come alive in the heart of every man. I hope you are eager to begin to pursue God's plans for you and your world in a new way. We are to be men who are godly examples of who we were created to be and who we can be.

Jesus was passionate about His calling to be about His Father's business. It consumed and motivated Him; He was driven to do only those things that pleased His Father. How about you? Does your passion cause you to go against the grain and stand up for God, even if it means being unpopular and challenged? Does your passion move you to take definitive action to reach your goals, even if it goes against what you've known all your life?

The Maasai demonstrate this passion in their relentless approach to life. Traditionally, they have depended on their cattle as their primary source of income, but due to drought and economic fluctuations, they have also been forced into farming. Their adjustment to growing vegetables is symbolic of doing whatever is necessary to continue growing as a people.

While some vegetables like onions and carrots grow beneath the soil, others such as tomatoes grow above the ground. To grow vertically, tomatoes must have external support like stakes or cages. By way of analogy, we don't want to be like the carrot—men growing unseen, unappreciated, and burrowing deeper underground. We want to be like the tomato—men who are visible, respected, and climbing higher toward the sky. But to grow, we have to climb. And to climb, like the tomato, we need a solid support system. That support system materializes when we harness our untapped power.

Men, we are being challenged to safeguard the posterity of masculinity. To achieve this goal and to access the untapped power of a man, we must align ourselves with the principles contained within the pages of this book.

1. The ***pervasion***. It is imperative that we seek a personal relationship with God the Father and let it pervade everything else in our lives.

2. The ***priority***. With calendars full of meetings, events, responsibilities, and activities, our priorities too often get misplaced. This generally means that pursuing a relationship with God the Father is either disrupted or not given any significance. Each day you must place a premium on cultivating a relationship with God by reading His Word and praying.

3. The ***parent***. We learn from our spiritual children, Manasseh and Ephraim. Two of the most powerful lessons they teach us are don't let your memory of past wrongs cause you to focus on retaliation, and don't let hard times suspend the continuous activity needed to propel you into greatness.

4. The ***plan***. You must demonstrate willingness to assume responsibility for your personal and family affairs. Take inventory of the areas in your life that have been neglected, and put energy behind making them better.

5. The *provider*. As a husband, father, or surrogate to others, we have a nonoptional responsibility to provide for those under our care. This requires that we consider others' needs before our own. It is the epitome of a selfless act that will yield great dividends.

6. The *promoter*. You should be a source of encouragement and have a tender heart for your family and the people within your community to help them become all that God intended them to be.

7. The *play*. There is unity and power in numbers. When men passionately collaborate and move toward a common goal, we exponentially increase our individual and collective potential to change the world.

8. The *protector*. Throughout history, men have protected their families and communities from natural and spiritual attacks. As men, we were designed to provide a security blanket of protection from the onslaught of the enemy.

9. The *producer*. Men should constantly be making progress toward improving the quality of life for their families and communities. Develop a results-oriented mentality that will provide you with the drive needed to no longer be just a consumer, but a producer as well.

10. The *professor*. This role will fulfill your responsibility of being a catalyst of learning. Men, we are to inspire and motivate our families, friends, and those whom we mentor to pursue lifelong learning. To accomplish this, we must be open

to learning and growing in areas in our own
lives that need development.

11. The *priest*. You are to search the scriptures diligently and seek ways to apply them to your life.
The benefits of your scriptural study and application are to be shared with your family and
friends. This will also inject a healthy reverence
into those we encounter for who God is and
why we must have a personal relationship with
Him.

12. The *prophet*. As men, it is our privileged opportunity to be a mouthpiece of truth to everyone
we encounter. This means being willing to share
the truth of God's Word with others. By dem-
onstrating a spirit of transparency as you live
out the Word of God, you solidify the foundation of your relationships with family and
friends and increase the probability that they
will embrace your vision.

13. The *pattern*. Men must always remember the
critical responsibility of being a role model for
their families and communities. This is particularly true when it comes to children, who are
more likely to model the behavior they observe.
Welcome this position, and begin to have a positive impact on someone's life.

The keys contained within the chapters of this book will
allow you to access the untapped power of a man, each one
building on the next. It's a matter of progressively becoming
what God intended you to be and being a part of elevating
men back to the status and position established from the
beginning of time.

So the personal question I will leave you with is, "How

much time are you willing to invest in yourself?" The reason for this question is twofold:

1. First, the one thing man is incapable of producing is time. Unless God intervenes, no man can add one second to a day. And because time is a scare resource, you must decide how it will be allocated. How much time will you set aside each day to develop and access your untapped power? You must make an honest assessment of your needs, followed by the use of the Calls to Action at the end of each chapter.

2. Second, the amount of time you spend on self-development will have a direct impact on your personal achievement. How far are you willing to go to obtain Godly success? Using only one or two of the principles in this book is akin to walking in ankle-high water.

> The keys contained within the chapters of this book will allow you to access the untapped power of a man, each one building on the next. It's a matter of progressively becoming what God intended you to be and being a part of elevating men back to the status and position established from the beginning of time.

It is my prayer that you be willing to launch into the deep and embrace all that this book has to offer. In the end, the untapped power you access will produce immeasurable blessings for your family, church, and community.

NOTES AND REFERENCES

CHAPTER 2: THE PROBLEM

1. M. Munroe, *Understanding the Purpose and Power of Men* (study guide), New Kensington, PA: Whitaker House, 2003.
2. Larry Ray Hafley, "Tolerate, Then Embrace," *BassFishing.com*, http://www.bassfishing.org/thebiblespeaks/Articles/FalseTeachings/Divides/tolerate.htm.
3. Jessie L. Krienert, "Masculinity and Crime: A Quantitative Exploration of Messerschmidt's Hypothesis," *Sociology.com*, 2003, http://www.sociology.org/content/vol7.2/01_krienert.html.
4. Morris M., "Ten Examples of Men's Issues the Media Love to Ignore," *ListVerse.com*, June 25, 2013, http://listverse.com/2013/06/25/10-examples-of-men39s-issues-the-media-loves-to-ignore/.
5. M. Munroe, Ibid.
6. John Eldredge, *Wild at Heart: Discovering the Secret of a Man's Soul*, Nashville, TN: Thomas Nelson, 2011.
7. Robert Hicks and John Trent, *The Masculine Journey: Understanding the Six Stages of Manhood*, Carol Stream, IL: NavPress Publishing, 1993.
8. Tim Elmore, "LeBron James: The Four Stages of Manhood," *GrowingLeaders.com*, July 15, 2014, http://growingleaders.com/blog/lebron-james-four-stages-manhood/.
9. Dr. Jawanza Kunjufu, *Developing Strong Black Male Ministries*, Sauk Village, IL: African American Images, 2006.

CHAPTER 3: THE PINNACLE

1. Chantelle Hunte, *The Power in Me: Ten Days of Feeling Good*, Raleigh, NC: Lulu Press, Inc., 2014.

CHAPTER 4: THE PROCESS

1. "Having a Sense of Purpose May Add Years to Your Life," May 12, 2014, *ScienceDaily.com*, http://www.sciencedaily.com/releases/2014/05/140512124308.htm.
2. James Strong and Robert L. Thomas, *The Strongest NASB Exhaustive Concordance*, Grand Rapids, MI: Zondervan Bible Publishers, 2004.

CHAPTER 6: THE PLAN

1. Ron Powers, *Mark Twain: A Life*, New York: Simon & Schuster, 2008.
2. *God's Little Devotional Book for Men*. Colorado Springs, CO: Honor Books, 1996.
3. Booker T. Washington, *Up from Slavery*. New York: Doubleday, 1901.
4. Carol Kuykendall and Elisa Morgan, *What Every Child Needs: Meet Your Child's Nine Basic Needs for Love*, Nashville, TN: Zondervan, 2013.
5. Simon Paige, *The Very Best of Winston Churchill: Quotes from a British Legend*. CreateSpace Publishing, 2014.
6. John Eldredge, ibid.
7. "Listening Dads," *ListenersUnite*, http://listenersunite.com/Quotes/Dads_Quotes.
8. C. W. Loritts, Jr., *Never Walk Away*, Chicago: Moody Press, 1997.

CHAPTER 7: THE PROVIDER

1. Les T. Csorba, *Trust: The One Thing That Makes or Breaks a Leader*, Nashville, TN: Thomas Nelson, Inc., 2004.
2. James C. Dobson, *The Complete Marriage and Family Home Reference Guide*, Carol Stream, IL: Tyndale House Publishers, 2000.

CHAPTER 8: THE PROMOTER

1. "Address of Carl Sandburg before the Joint Session of Congress," February 2, 1959, *NPS.gov*, http://www.nps.gov/carl/learn/historyculture/upload/Address-of-Carl-Sandburg-before-the-Joint-Session-of-Congress.pdf.
2. Sue Skeen, *BoardOfWisdom.com*, http://boardofwisdom.com/togo/Quotes/ShowQuote?msgid=6472#.Vh6En_lViko.
3. "Martyn Lloyd-Jones Quotes," *ChristianQuotes.info*, http://www.christianquotes.info/quotes-by-author/martyn-lloyd-jones-quotes/.

CHAPTER 10: THE PROTECTOR

1. "Strength Quotes," *MotivatingQuotes.com*, http://www.motivatingquotes.com/strength.htm.

2. "Martin Luther King, Jr., Quotes," *BrainyQuotes.com*, http://www.brainyquote.com/quotes/quotes/m/martinluth103526.html.

3. John Henry Newman, *Selected Sermons, Prayers, and Devotions*, New York: Vintage Books, 1999.

4. "Stream of Consciousness," *GAIAMLife blog*, http://blog.gaiam.com/quotes/authors/phillips-brooks.

5. "George Walker Bush," *God & Country*, http://www.god-and-country.info/GWBush.html.

CHAPTER 11: THE PRODUCER

1. Douglas Quenqua, "Study Finds Spatial Skill is Early Sign of Creativity," July 15, 2013, *The New York Times*, http://www.nytimes.com/2013/07/16/us/study-finds-early-signs-of-creativity-in-adults.html.

2. "Procrastination," *Wikipedia*, https://en.wikipedia.org/wiki/Procrastination.

3. Piers Steel, PhD, *The Procrastination Equation: How to Stop Putting Things Off and Start Getting Stuff Done*, Toronto, Ontario, Canada: Random House Canada, 2010.

4. Hara Estroff Marano, "Why We Procrastinate," July 1 2005, *Psychology Today*, https://www.psychologytoday.com/articles/200507/why-we-procrastinate.

5. Mark O'Connell, *The Good Father: On Men, Masculinity, and Life in the Family*, New York: Simon & Schuster, 2015.

CHAPTER 13: THE PRIEST

1. William J. Federer, Douglas MacArthur's Father of the Year Speech, 1942, http://www.americanminute.com/index.php?date=01-26.

CHAPTER 15: THE PATTERN

1. "Remarks on Becoming Prime Minister (St Francis's Prayer)," *Margaret Thatcher Foundation*, http://www.margaretthatcher.org/document/104078.

2. Danita Whyte and Daniella Whyte, *Dear Papa: Letters to My Father*, Joshua, TX: Torch Legacy Publications, 2009.

3. David Young, *Breakthrough Power for Athletes: A Daily Guide to an Extraordinary Life*, Round Rock, TX: Wind Runner Press, 2012.

4. "Stream of Consciousness," *GAIAMLife blog*, http://blog.gaiam.com/quotes/authors/harold-g-hillam.

5. "Father Quotes and Sayings," *BestSayingsQuotes.com*, http://www.bestsayingsquotes.com/quote/my-father-gave-me-the-greatest-gift-anyone-could-812.html.

IF YOU'RE A FAN OF THIS BOOK, PLEASE TELL OTHERS...

- Write about *The Untapped Power of a Man* on your blog, Facebook and Twitter

- Suggest the book to your friends, co-workers, neighbors and family

- When you're in a bookstore, ask them if they carry the book.

- This book is available through all major distributors, any bookstore that does not have this book can easily stock it!

- Write a positive review of *The Untapped Power of a Man* via www.amazon.com

- Purchase additional copies to give away as gifts.

- Visit: www.untappedpowerofaman.com

To order additional copies contact us:
HigherLife Publishing and Marketing
PO Box 623307
Oviedo, FL 32765
or email: info@ahigherlife.com

NATIONS FORD COMMUNITY CHURCH

WRITE THE VISION. MAKE IT PLAIN.

Our vision is to be a regional full-service church, Strengthening families; Teaching the Word of God; Advancing the Kingdom of God; Reaching People and Serving our communities.

Our strategy is to occupy the region by developing the Nations Ford Community Village and shine as stars for the glory of God through acts of love and service both locally and globally.

FAMILY MINISTRIES

CHRISTIAN EDUCATION

MISSIONS & OUTREACH

WORSHIP, ARTS MUSIC

CONGREGATIONAL CARE

www.nationsford.org